After Obama

Barack Obama's foreign policy has failed but the American strategic mind has not yet closed. In *After Obama,* Robert S. Singh examines how and why US global influence has weakened and contributed to the erosion of the world America made, endangering international order and liberal values. A well-intentioned but naïve strategy of engagement has encouraged US adversaries such as Russia, China and Iran to assert themselves while allowing Western alliances to fray. However, challenging the claims of an inevitable American decline, Singh argues that US leadership is a matter of will as much as wallet. Despite partisan polarization and populist anger at home, and the rise of the rest abroad, Washington can renew American leadership and – through a New American Internationalism – pave a path to the restoration of global order. Timely and provocative, the book offers a powerful critique of the Obama Doctrine's pre-mortem on American power and a call for strategic resolution in place of "leading from behind."

After Obama is Robert Singh's tenth book, his second on Obama's foreign policy, and follows books on *The Bush Doctrine and the War on Terrorism, Governing America, The Congressional Black Caucus* and *The Farrakhan Phenomenon.* His previous coauthored book for Cambridge, *After Bush,* won the 2009 Richard E. Neustadt Prize of the American Politics Group of the United Kingdom for the best book on US politics written by a non-US author in the previous twelve months. A critical review of *Barack Obama's Post-American Foreign Policy* in the *Claremont Review of Books* in 2014 described Singh as an "intimate" of the US foreign policy establishment.

After Obama

*Renewing American Leadership,
Restoring Global Order*

ROBERT S. SINGH
University of London

CAMBRIDGE
UNIVERSITY PRESS

CAMBRIDGE
UNIVERSITY PRESS

32 Avenue of the Americas, New York NY 10013

Cambridge University Press is part of the University of Cambridge.

It furthers the University's mission by disseminating knowledge in the pursuit of education, learning and research at the highest international levels of excellence.

www.cambridge.org
Information on this title: www.cambridge.org/9781107142480

© Robert S. Singh, 2016

First published 2016

Printed in the United States of America by Sheridan Books, Inc.

A catalog record for this publication is available from the British Library

Library of Congress Cataloging in Publication data
Names: Singh, Robert, author.
Title: After Obama : renewing American leadership, restoring global order / Robert S. Singh.
Description: Cambridge; New York : Cambridge University Press, [2016] | Includes bibliographical references and index.
Identifiers: LCCN 2016003552 | ISBN 9781107142480 (hardback) | ISBN 9781316507261 (pbk.)
Subjects: LCSH: United States – Foreign relations – 21st century. | World politics – 21st century.
Classification: LCC JZ1480.S49 2016 | DDC 327.73–dc23
LC record available at http://lccn.loc.gov/2016003552

ISBN 978-1-107-14248-0 Hardback
ISBN 978-1-316-50726-1 Paperback

To Barbara

With love, thanks and admiration

Contents

Figures and tables

Figures

Tables

I

A return to strategy

13 NOTES p.131

Barack Obama's foreign policy has failed, but the American strategic mind has not yet closed. For the United States, the West and the cause of liberal democracy, the years since 2009 have comprised a succession of defeats, reversals and missed opportunities. Obama's presidency has left America weaker and the world more unstable than when he entered the White House. With few accomplishments, declining influence and diminished credibility, a dysfunctional Washington is in retreat, strategically adrift of its allies and a fading force to its foes. The principles governing the exercise of US power have become opaque, contributing to the fragmentation of a once robust liberal international order. Abdicating clear and decisive leadership has advanced the rise of serious threats to the security and prosperity of the world America made. Obama's presidency has been historic and perhaps transformational, but for all the wrong reasons. The United States and the West urgently require a return to strategy: the renewal of genuine American leadership and, thereby, a path to the restoration of global order.

After Obama makes a case for how this may come about. Obama's immense promise has proven illusory. Instead of affirming America's singular place in the world, the president allowed the world to redefine and diminish it for him. The leadership lacuna has ceded influence to Washington's adversaries. But neither polarized politics at home nor premature obituaries of the late, great United States preclude the revival of American power. The next president can reverse what the Obama administration has wrought, to advance in its place a grand strategy more firmly anchored in US interests and ideals. Informed less by nostalgia for nonexistent golden eras than a cautious confidence and, even, hope, the following pages assess what Obama got wrong, anticipate efforts to put matters right and offer an argument for change that America and its allies can believe in: a New American Internationalism in the service of a Second American Century.

The other great recession

President Obama claimed in his 2012 State of the Union address that, "Anyone who tells you that America is in decline or that our influence has waned, doesn't know what they're talking about.①On the core metrics of national power, he was correct: America is not declining. But this is more despite than because of Obama's foreign policies. Moreover, contrary to his assertion, the United States' global influence is in deep recession. Ask whether the mullahs in Tehran, the Politburo in Beijing and the Putin mafia in Moscow will welcome or regret the Obama administration's passing and the answer is self-explanatory. In geopolitics, an invariably wise strategy is to do what your rivals least favor. All too often, Obama charted the opposite course. America's global leadership balance is in the red as a result.

Geopolitical influence is an expression of power effectively employed and an attribute of successful national leadership: getting others to do what you want them to do. Leadership is the mediating force fusing abstract power, as resources, into effective power, as influence: the strategic capacity to set agendas and tactical nous to persuade or coerce others to go along. By definition, powerless countries cannot lead. But through choice or indecision, a powerful nation can fail to lead. Such has been Obama's America. An audit of global power confirms that while the American nation-state remains strong – the preeminent military, economic, diplomatic and cultural force on earth by a distance – its influence is waning as destructive anti-American forces wax worldwide.

Negative evaluations of the president may appear harsh or premature, driven by reflexive partisanship or worse. But even as a non-American and nonpartisan – not least a Brit all too conscious of his own nation's ignominious retreat from global leadership and the "littler England" it heralds – criticism is unavoidable. A decent respect to the opinions of America compels the observation that, with the best will in the world, finding examples of Obama's strategic success is a fool's errand. Obama did not brand his time in government with outstanding acts of statesmanship. Instead, well-intentioned but naïve efforts to recast US leadership and set in motion a new set of global understandings have proven mistaken and costly. America may not have suffered the humiliations abroad of Jimmy Carter's presidency. Nor has Obama been responsible for a specific blunder on the scale of Vietnam or the occupation of Iraq. However, although less obviously calamitous, the retrograde consequences of strategic retreat are at least as profound.

After the George W. Bush era, "leading from behind" appealed strongly to Democratic Party activists and an anxious public troubled by domestic strife. But Obama's multiple failings as the free world's leader compromised the pursuit of the national interest, leaving America increasingly ineffectual. From the egregious refusal to enforce redlines in Syria to the vacillating responses to Russian expansionism and Chinese provocations in Asia, a risk-averse

Washington appears unable to shape – much less impose discipline upon – international relations. Worse still, it has frequently seemed unwilling even to try. Admittedly, in a defeatist fashion, Obama's defining down of US foreign policy through negatives has been audacious. Abandoning the constructive ambition that historically informed grand strategy, his administration made clear everything that America will *not* do: deploy ground troops, determine deadlines by strategic rather than political needs, commit adequate resources beyond artificially constrained means, act decisively without the support of others or promote a balance of power favoring freedom. Overwhelmed by limits, both self-imposed and real, America appears unconscious of possibilities. Clear in the abstract about what it disapproves, the United States equivocates as to what it concretely stands for. Ambivalent about partners while credulous of adversaries, Obama's pivot to America – the prioritizing of a progressive policy agenda at home – has underpinned retrenchment, retreat and accommodation abroad.

As America's national debt has inexorably risen, the accompanying leadership deficit has left allies estranged while encouraging state and nonstate adversaries to challenge the basic norms of established order. Only the myopic could view the international system as one characterized by the "mutual respect" and shared interests so frequently venerated by the president. Rather, in place of international law and order, instability and disequilibria fester. A "broken windows" world has emerged in which rules are solemnly invoked but unenforced, fine-sounding principles idealized but undefended and professorial speeches substituted for effective diplomacy – with international law reverentially treated not as a complement to geopolitical leadership but the superior alternative. "Moral leadership is more powerful than any weapon," Obama declared in 2009. But the perilous results of his statecraft strongly suggest otherwise.

Setting out to advance "global zero," Obama has instead paved the path to nuclear proliferation. Attempting to "reset" relations, Russian bellicosity has been emboldened, shifting regional and global dynamics, with Moscow's largest rearmament and territorial expansion since the Soviet Union's collapse, a sharp contrast to America's strategic withdrawal. Pledging not to increase the US nuclear arsenal while repeatedly disavowing the use of conventional force, American defense spending is on a trajectory inverse to multiplying threats – declining to just 2.9 percent of gross domestic product by 2017, its lowest level for fifty years, and posing a growing danger to national security. The post-Cold War security order and a Europe "whole and free" are threatened by a resurgent Russia intent on recreating a lost empire. While supposedly "pivoting" to Asia, Washington's Pacific allies perceive an absent America bereft of strategic resolve, as Beijing more than ever competes aggressively across the full spectrum of power with a United States it sees as dedicated to, but incapable of, thwarting its rise. Reaching out to the world's 1.6 billion Muslims, America remains no more popular today under Obama – and in some Muslim nations even less so – than his predecessor. The president who undeclared the war on terror to depart the Middle East for good has reluctantly returned, with Islamism spreading and sectarian conflicts raging uncontained. As US interventions in Libya and Yemen leave in their wake civil wars and terrorist havens, nonintervention in Syria fuels genocide, refugee crises and regional conflagration. Washington enables the dominance of theocratic Iran while unnerving democratic Israel as a four-decades-old regional order disintegrates. And having prematurely claimed al Qaeda's decimation, its meta-stasized offshoots compete with an even more brutal death cult, ISIS – in failed and failing states from Afghanistan to Algeria – for the dubious privilege of returning the Middle East, Africa and South Asia to the seventh century and attacking the West through growing franchises of Islamist terror.

In this interdependent world, Las Vegas rules are inapplicable: what happens in one region no longer stays there. Yet US strategy appears fatalist and reactive, that of a bemused bystander. America's fading authority is regarded with resignation by allies no longer counting on Washington and contempt by adversaries neither respectful nor fearful of US power. The outsourcing of foreign policy has been a futile exercise in irresponsibility and ineffectiveness. Less the indispensable nation than a "dispensable" power by turns irresolute and irrelevant, Washington's unhappy reward for its frantic oscillation between engagement and disengagement is a diminished capacity to influence matters on the ground and the authoring of its own exit from critical theaters. Rarely has so little been accomplished for the investment of so much ineffectual diplomacy. Being apologetic about American power has not made Moscow or Beijing more compliant. Appeasing Iran has not altered its ambitions. Self-denigration about past sins has not pacified jihadists from Paris to Boston. Outside the United States – not least in China – Obama's tenure is regarded as the inflection point in a downward American spiral, ripe for exploitation and an epochal moment for international order. In trying to manage a world wary of US power but desperate for leadership, Obama has advanced the unravelling of global order to hasten the arrival of a "post-American" world that he purportedly sought to delay.

Because of Obama's strategic sabbatical, America's credibility is doubted and its entreaties disregarded. The resulting dimensions of the erosion of influence extend far and wide, to the detriment of world order and endangering of liberal values. It is not merely the United States that has been poorly served by policies rendering it an increasingly parochial power – the ageing global policeman opting for a more comfortable desk job for want of apparent criminals – but its allies as well. Not since the Cold War has collective security confronted so many concurrent threats. The future of the world's most successful military alliance, the North Atlantic Treaty Organization (NATO), hangs by a thread, with US defense cuts abetting feckless European disarmament. The West's decades-long military edge is drawing to a dangerous end. The Pentagon has abandoned the commitment to be able to wage two major wars simultaneously; some question its capacity to emerge victorious even in one. The fabric of alliances is fraying. US security guarantees ring increasingly hollow, their atrophy awakening long-dormant regional security competitions and encouraging a risk-laden freelancing liable to ignite new conflicts.

At the same time, adversaries no longer fear American disfavor. Russia, China, Iran and North Korea perceive diplomatic indecision and military timidity. And while they repeatedly launch cyber-attacks against America and rearm for conflict, US forces remain ill-prepared, insufficiently resourced and inadequately configured to defend national interests and discharge global responsibilities. Underinvestment in the military and overinvestment in global cooperation has left America with more international challenges but fewer capabilities to meet them. Obama has violated the presidential equivalent of the Hippocratic Oath, to not harm America's standing – a curious achievement for a president whose supposed conceptual lodestar for foreign policy was "don't do stupid shit."ⓘ   /3/

But the weakness here is, ultimately, not so much military as political. The troubling reality about American power is altogether new: that with threats multiplying, the United States is increasingly unwilling or unable to assume the lead in providing global governance, guaranteeing public goods and underwriting international security. Disdainful of "discretionary" wars, America in retreat is instead accepting of strategic defeats of choice. The international system is growing more fissiparous. Deterrence is weakening. Allies are vulnerable. Non-Western states' nuclear arsenals are expanding, with their ranks set to grow, most disturbingly in an imploding Middle East. Existential threats on the USSR's scale may be a thing of the past, but fearsome new ones from cyber-warfare to biological weapons and mass fatality terrorism are increasing their reach. The "doomsday clock" – an indicator of perceived proximity to global catastrophe, developed by the Bulletin of Atomic Scientists – now stands at three minutes to midnight, for the first time since the Cuban Missile Crisis of 1962.ⓘ   /3/

At least as significant, the ranks of those who would consign the West's civilization to oblivion are growing within and without, while Western self-confidence languishes at a low ebb. Our collective political compass – the shared sense of who we are – is in flux. Under the Obama administration, ideological battles are no longer joined but abandoned on altars of a world-weary *realpolitik* and nebulous moral relativism. Clarion calls for freedom and democracy – a strategic leitmotif from Woodrow Wilson to George W. Bush – have been silenced. Confronted by nihilism and barbarism, such values no longer appear universally valid, even as the president persists in bearing witness to a fictional global order based on shared beliefs. But the norms of power have proven more compelling than the power of norms. The world is becoming safer not for democracy but for authoritarianism and less, not more, respectful of international laws, universal rules and common values. Obama enjoys quoting Martin Luther King's optimistic declaration that, "The arc of the moral universe is long, but it bends toward justice." History's incline, however, suggests that recent decades have been a precious aberration in the destructive annals of great power war. Forgotten among presidential paeans to international comity and community is the most timeless inconvenient truth: "If you want peace, prepare for war."

The sheer scale of the administration's fluency in failure is thus remarkable. Judged by the ambitious standards Obama set as a candidate, his foreign affairs management has failed. Assessed by allies' confidence and adversaries' fears, the most elementary national security tests have been flunked. Most importantly, evaluated in terms of the parameters of successful policy – whether US vital interests are better secured and global influence more advanced by the end of a president's term than the outset – the Obama experiment has backfired. In seeking to depart from decades of America's strategic culture, mistaken assumptions, misconceived priorities and misguided tactics have yielded a more turbulent world and a downgraded US power. A candidate who reached the White House intent upon entering the history books as the ultimate peace president will depart, not with the "tide of war" receding – as Obama assured in 2011 – but advancing. Cynics can be forgiven for estimating the greatest recession of recent years to have been in American leadership. The problematic legacy bequeathed the forty-fifth president is one requiring extensive remedial action to recover lost ground, reestablish US strength, and stabilize a world in dangerous disorder.

Audacity exhausted: American disengagement

Obama assumed office with unprecedented goodwill. Within America, the symbolism of his election – racial, generational and ideological – was profound. Outside, after years of growing anti-Americanism, the "un-Bush" was welcomed almost everywhere with relief. Political elites around the world were anxious for good relations while mass publics anticipated bold acts on the international stage. To those for whom the Bush era had instilled a false sense of national insecurity wherein perceived threats – from terrorism and weapons of mass destruction to outlaw states – were "overblown," Obama represented the avatar of rationality and threat deflation. His promise was to implement long-held progressive beliefs that US policy was too militarized and Manichean, where a more diplomatic, less strident approach would entice reciprocal concessions on the part of adversaries. The award of the Nobel Peace Prize – in essence, for not being his predecessor – represented an early manifestation of cosmopolitan credulity: "we are the ones we have been waiting for."

The core to Obama's approach was "strategic engagement," a mission to "detoxify" America's image and a message for its enemies, that "We will extend a hand if you are willing to unclench your fist." Engagement, "the active participation of the United States in relationships beyond our borders" as defined by the National Security Strategy (NSS) document of 2010, would repair the broken Bush years. Through the force multipliers of moral example, demonstrations of good intent and diplomatic outreach, steady progress toward a global constitution of sorts could advance. Not all nations would progress at the same pace, some proving reluctant rather than responsible. But a pragmatic concordat, a global "buy-in," could nonetheless be reached through goodwill and accommodation. As Obama stressed in Prague in April 2009, "Rules must be binding. Violations must be punished. Words must mean something."⑤ In [3] 2015, the president even defined the "Obama Doctrine": "The doctrine is: We will engage, but we preserve all our capabilities."⑥ Though accompanied by /3/ calculated risks, engagement represented a better bet than coercive diplomacy, ostracizing enemies or resort to force.

Disregarding for the moment why Obama took the opposite view toward apartheid South Africa in the 1980s – when concerted isolation rather than "constructive engagement" was the progressive preference – the results of this conciliatory approach appear meager. True, the fists of Cuba and Myanmar have partially unclenched, promising modest gains in sclerotic states peripheral to US vital interests. But where those interests are seriously in play, Russian and Chinese fists appear even more tightly compressed and ostentatiously punching across Eurasia, the Near East and the Pacific Rim. As for Iran, the administration's marquee example of success, the jury's verdict at best remains "not proven," despite the administration offering less an olive branch than entire forest for a nuclear accord. In short, Obama's approach has yielded modest results where they are least consequential, and rebuffs and capitulation where they matter most. From Tehran's serial violations of UN Security Council resolutions through Moscow's "hybrid" wars and Syrian intervention to China's man-made militarized islands in contested waters, rules have been unbinding, violations unpunished and words have meant – *Alice in Wonderland*-like – whatever the user wished. No geopolitical Rubicon has been crossed. In place of a zero tolerance for aggression is indulgence. Mendacity met hope, and mendacity prevailed while, like King Canute ordering the waves to cease in order to demonstrate his own powerlessness, the president solemnly observed to the UN General Assembly in September 2015 that, "we, the nations of the world, cannot return to the old ways of conflict and coercion."⑦   /3/

Critics might object that a fair accounting should factor in Obama's obvious good intentions, intelligence and sincere commitment to outreach. But many of the same critics tend, rightly, to depict geopolitics as akin to chess or poker. Positive intentions count for nothing in assessing risk and reward, calling bluffs and steadily prevailing. "Diplomania" has its limits, not least when, executed poorly, its signal accomplishment is racking up more air miles than accomplishments. Where engagement was initially most energetically expounded (Russia, China), it has been rebuffed. Where most necessary (the Arab uprisings, Syria, Ukraine) it was least apparent. Where most doggedly pursued despite its manifest dangers (Iran), its outcome appears chronically destabilizing and based on a geopolitical framework that collapsed almost as soon as it was concluded. "Smart" power? Ironically, engagement was a singularly inapt misnomer for

the rank mismanagement of alliance relations. When even a sympathetic out-
let like *The Economist* observes that, "many foreigners would welcome an
American commander-in-chief who is genuinely engaged with the world outside America," the substance and smartness of "engagement" can legitimately
be called into questions[8]

Although tempting to dismiss the Obama Doctrine as comprising so little
conviction that none could disagree with it, the president's error was not a failure to understand the power of ideas, but rather, which ideas work. Skeptics
might suggest Obama is only the latest president to fall into this trap. Realists
have long lamented US strategy's lack of an anchor in a sense of history or
geopolitics and bemoaned Americans' reluctance to recognize global affairs as
a remorseless competition for advantage among states. Animated by America's
liberal political culture, US leaders have instead envisioned foreign policy as a
teleological struggle for justice rather than a "permanent endeavor for contingent aims," however much legitimacy and values remain important elements
of grand strategy[9]

But Obama departed decisively from his predecessors. It was not simply
Obama's reluctance to take more than rhetorical stands on human rights, rejection of support for democratic movements and reticence about military force.
What was truly unprecedented was his belief in a strategic alchemy premised
on a quixotic form of exemplarism: that other states' behavior hinges on prior
demonstrations of US good faith. Obama has seemingly been convinced that
conflict arises not primarily from adversaries who comprehend each other's
irreconcilable ambitions all too accurately but from misunderstandings that
American conciliatoriness can transform into cooperation. Yet the misunderstanding is entirely Obama's.

The mismatch between presidential rhetoric and reality has found expression across foreign and national security policies. Where John F. Kennedy
pledged America to "support any friend, oppose any foe," Obama's assistance
was transactional and his opposition negotiable. Where Ronald Reagan's Cold
War strategy was bracingly straightforward ("We win; they lose"), Obama's
instead conveyed the impression of an insular force keen to reinvent itself at
home by downsizing abroad; there was no "they." Adversaries were merely
pliable partners-to-be whom America had yet to persuade. The measuring rod
for US credibility was less a commitment to internationalism than diplomatic
maximalism and military minimalism, whether to end chemical attacks on
innocent civilians or lend lethal aid to sovereign democracies under foreign
assault.

Such has been the Obama administration's conviction that diplomacy can
change circumstances on the ground – rather than circumstances typically
establishing the limits of diplomacy – that it is difficult even to comprehend
the president's approach to nonproliferation without prioritizing America's
prior good faith. The first recommendation Obama made in Prague was for
the United States to set a positive example by cutting its nuclear arsenal, which

would afford the requisite moral authority to persuade Iran not to develop nuclear weapons. But no evidence existed that US reductions alter the calculus of states contemplating going nuclear. The American arsenal has been reduced by 80 percent since 1991. Yet the North Korean, Pakistani and Iranian pursuit of nuclear capabilities intensified. Only when adversarial regimes have toppled, feared change or fallen under the US nuclear umbrella have they willingly disarmed. Foreign leaders base decisions about nuclear weaponry on their perceived strategic needs, not in response to disarmament. To imagine otherwise is merely to invite forces inimical to America to grow.

The president can more easily be forgiven for not anticipating seismic events such as the Arab uprisings. Even here, however, less forgivable were the twin failures of ignoring intelligence advice about looming threats – most notably ISIS – and refusing to respond effectively once the direction of change became clear: to play the hand he was dealt as well as possible, from pressuring Iraq into accepting an American presence that could serve US strategic interests to delinking Syria from the accommodation of Iran. Instead, Obama appeared to have morphed from a Shakespearean "lean and hungry" Cassius into a Hamlet-like figure suffering what psychologists term "overchoice": confronted with so many options that whittling them down to a single one was more stressful than giving up altogether. In this, as in so much, the administration's policy reflected less a sober assessment of geopolitical risks than the compelling domestic electoral imperative for a progressive president to distance himself from his predecessor's militarism. But if no appetite existed for influencing the direction and pace of events on the ground from Syria to Ukraine, a more honest approach would have acknowledged both realities rather than offer cosmetic interventions of minimal benefit.

The defining moment in the shrinking of US influence came in the fall of 2013 with the confusion over, and ultimately the abandonment of, using force against Assad. The climb-down confirmed administration redlines as less solid than the French Maginot Line against the Wehrmacht in the 1930s, but similarly ineffective, reassuring Russia, China and Iran that the United States would talk loudly but carry only the smallest of sticks. Until 2014, when Americans turned their attention to ISIS, one could perhaps make the case that Obama's aversion to military force synchronized with his core constituency and public opinion. But responsible governing requires defining interests and values and demonstrating the will to defend them. Obama simply refused to shape opinion. There are few examples in the history of any nation advancing its interests by dodging tough decisions or outsourcing leadership. Admittedly, the price of intervention was always uncertain in Syria. But the price of nonintervention has been brutally clear: an uncontained war whose spillover engulfed not only neighboring states but also nations far beyond. The Syrian debacle confirmed the credibility gap in Obama's promises and weakening of US security guarantees. As the president asked in the aftermath of the regime's chemical attacks, "If we won't enforce accountability in the face of this heinous act, what does it say about our resolve to stand up to others who flout fundamental rules? To governments who would choose to build nuclear weapons? To terrorists who would spread biological weapons? To armies who carry out genocide?'[10]

What, indeed, Mr. President?

American adversaries received the message loud and clear. After two years of serial US concessions, nuclear defiance was rewarded and Iranian influence is on the march across the Arab Middle East. As former secretaries of state Henry Kissinger and George Shultz noted, "negotiations that began 12 years ago as an international effort to prevent an Iranian capability to develop a nuclear arsenal are ending with an agreement that concedes this very capability."[11] For fifteen years, Tehran will never be further than one year from a nuclear weapon. Thereafter, it will be substantially closer. The threat of war now constrains the West more than Iran and, in the inevitable event of Iranian violations, the remote prospects for reimposing sanctions will primarily isolate Washington, not Tehran. Absent a new US strategic approach, the nuclear pact will reinforce rather than resolve the region's challenges. Far from coolly assessing the risk-reward ratio, the agreement represented a high-risk bet on a change of Iranian regime behavior that recklessly gambled the future of America's allies, the peace of the region and the wider world – one whose outcome Obama will not be around politically to pay during his lucrative post-presidency.

In legitimizing Tehran's ambitions, the deal also undermines nonproliferation efforts. In Prague, Obama had pledged "to seek the peace and security of a world without nuclear weapons," called for treaties to limit the weapons programs of established nuclear powers and reinforcing a faltering nonproliferation regime. Instead, with eyes wide shut, the White House rewarded Iran for persistent efforts to subvert that regime. The message to others was clear: even the most flagrant violations by the most dangerous regimes will not provoke a decisive US response. Failing to assuage their fears, the House of Saud is widely believed already to have made the strategic decision to secure its own arsenal, an outcome likely to encourage others – Egypt, Turkey – to create a poly-nuclear powder-keg. In seeking a capstone to his presidency, Obama has erected a tombstone to American influence in a region less crucial to US energy but ever vital to global prosperity and security.

What should other hostile powers infer? For the answer, we need not look far. Once unquestioned, American primacy is no longer assumed. Adversaries perceive a retreating power, uncomfortable with coercion and doubting its role. In Moscow, Putin seized on the opportunity to leverage maximum benefit to project Russian power, taking note of a military alliance – the North Atlantic Treaty Organization (NATO) – increasingly lacking an effective and interoperable military and a White House mystifyingly convinced that, "the measure of strength is no longer defined by the control of territory."[12] For the Chinese, Obama's presidency confirmed that American decline and China's ascent were occurring more rapidly than anticipated. The conspicuous collapse of US resolve was duly noted. As a result, through a series of unforced errors, Washington is unwittingly transforming rivals into enemies, encouraging assertiveness in place of caution, and emboldening gambling instead of inducing – rather than exhibiting – risk aversion. Outgunned in China's neighborhood and Russia's alike, while passively presiding over the disintegration of its post-1973 stabilizing role in the Middle East, "payback" for decades of dominance appears all too possible with a president who not only reluctantly accepts, but also actively welcomes, a diminished US role. Under Obama's singular version of the "American Pacifier," it is the United States that requires restraining, not others.

Of course, primacy was never a guarantee of influence. Before Obama, America could not easily dominate the international system. At the Cold War's height, with defense spending far greater than today, the United States did not secure military victories in Korea or Vietnam. Constructing a liberal order relied on ceding relative economic influence, rebuilding powers who would compete with America. And from the UK's refusal to participate in Vietnam and France's withdrawal from NATO in 1966 to German opposition to the Iraq War, even close allies have periodically refused to go along.

But if primacy never constituted a sufficient condition of influence, it was a necessary one. Some might contend that Obama's "strategic patience" is finally yielding dividends in his twilight. That Egypt, Turkey and Saudi Arabia expend blood and treasure to play military roles in the wars plaguing the Middle East offers a welcome departure from behind-the-scenes diplomacy. That India and Japan should assert themselves in Asia is surely positive. Pooling responsibility to police international order and deliver global public goods need not be inherently risky. Such assertiveness reflects, however, not a coordinated concert of conviction but a shared judgment about American retreat. An Israel, Saudi Arabia or Japan untethered from Washington is optimal neither from the perspective of US influence nor regional stability. Yet an imbalance in resolve, with genuine fears of Washington welching on its security promises, underlies the new assertiveness of clients who perceive no preferable alternatives with Obama in the White House. When a Gulf ally declines a president's invitation to a White House meeting two days before it is due, to attend a horse show near London (as Bahrain's King Khalifa did in May 2015), something is seriously amiss. It is an odd strategy of patience that exhausts allies but spurs adversaries and where US policies appear diminished rather than enhanced by presidential advocacy.

The Obama syndrome: retrenchment, retreat and accommodation

To resume the strategic offensive, America must overcome a new "syndrome" – not that of Vietnam or Iraq, but Obama. Allies have been bewildered by an administration paying reluctant lip service to "partners" while assiduously placating adversaries. Rivals have moved from puzzlement regarding the Obama

Doctrine's opaque logic to an appreciation of the president's pusillanimity. For more than seventy years, the United States followed foreign policies of global scope whose core feature was the ability and willingness to employ force to defend vital national interests. Now, with pin-pricks and postures substituting for policies, this is uncertain.

Whether or not Obama's approach owes more to conviction, convenience or legacy-hunting remains unclear. Defenders claim that use of the military refutes accusations of "softness" on national security. The increased deployment of drones and targeted assassination was a controversial feature of counterterrorism policy. Obama succeeded in killing Osama bin Laden where Bush failed. Important elements of the intelligence and surveillance architecture established under his predecessor were maintained. ISIS also faced air strikes in Syria and Iraq by US forces.

But Obama's success in "denigrating and destroying" Islamist terror has been an abject failure. The United States is losing the war against ISIS, which has become a growth enterprise with safe havens, financing and physical and virtual terror sanctuaries – the destruction of which was absolutely central to post-9/11 counterterrorism – spreading throughout the Middle East, Africa, South Asia and the Caucasus. Euphemisms from "overseas contingency operations" to "countering violent extremism" have not reduced Islamist ranks. By 2015, more than one thousand recruits from fifty nations traveled to join ISIS monthly, exceeding by a factor of ten the numbers at the height of the Iraq War a decade ago. And while aggressive use of drones has proven a vital instrument, Obama has failed to resolve the issues of tactics, law and morality of the kind that he once insisted relied on a false dichotomy between security and rights. "We reject as false the choice between our safety and our ideals," the president declared in his first inaugural. But the falsity was believing the two were separable even in principle, let alone practice.

Much of the limited military success Obama enjoyed also occurred under duress, subject to strenuous political rather than strategic considerations. Neither in Tel Aviv nor Tehran were Obama's claims of considering force to destroy Iran's nuclear program taken seriously. With every month of his presidency, the administration's core national security impetus became manifest: an unwillingness to employ America's military might where, when and how it really mattered. The opposition to using force to keep Iran from a nuclear arsenal even hinted at the possibility of fundamental change in US foreign policy. Few challenges compare to keeping nuclear weapons out of the hands of an aggressive, Islamist, anti-Western regime seeking hegemony in an energy-rich region on which the global economy depends. If employing force to defend such an interest has become unthinkable, then US foreign policy has entered a wholly new and disturbing era.

Even if this is not the case, international security is suffering. In 2012, global military spending declined by 0.5 percent, and for the first time since 1991, the US proportion of total spending fell below 40 percent. Defense expenditure has been cut 21 percent in real terms since 2011. Readiness is compromised. Yet, for the first time since the Cold War, the rest of the world's submarine fleet is growing. Russia's invasion of Ukraine in 2014 occurred when draw-downs to combat forces in Europe had removed the last American tanks from the continent (some 250 returned during 2014–15), with an army presence that numbered 210,000 and deployed 5,000 tanks at the end of the Cold War now comprising just two small brigade combat teams of some 30,000 troops in Germany and Italy. Frantic calls for reinforcing Poland and the Baltic states were met with the Lilliputian dispatch of a few hundred paratroopers.

Obama's supporters have often pointed to an understandable post-Bush war fatigue, the most dramatic expression of a broader exhaustion with global responsibilities. Candidate Obama had been elected to end two inherited wars, not commence new ones. A more restrained course appeared optimal. A president elected to end "dumb" wars, a weary superpower and defense cuts of one trillion dollars together created an entirely new type of military engagement with the world: drones over Pakistan, air strikes against ISIS, rump garrisons in Afghanistan and advisers in Iraq and Ukraine. Even these modest deployments represented more action than desired by the commander in chief. But with the presidential hand forced by the vacuum in Eurasian power left by the withdrawal of US ground troops on his own orders, the chaos following the Arab uprisings, Russia's meddling in a weak Ukraine and collapsing Syria, and an EU stubbornly determined to disarm and evade responsibility for its own security, the bare minimum of forward action was employed. In every instance of military force, Obama approved something less than sufficient to be transformative, politically permissible tools determining the mission rather than the mission compelling the selection of the relevant military tools. As a result, far from quelling the swelling impulse toward violence, wars beckon Obama's successor from almost all quarters of the globe.

But the US public ultimately appears less war weary than wary. Unlike Europe, where most citizens have been shaped by education and popular culture to be repulsed by war despite having no experience of it, history has afforded Americans different sensibilities. Americans remain not so much fatality – or casualty – as defeat-phobic. Moreover, with less than 1 percent of the US population serving in the military, exactly how much of a burden most have truly experienced is a matter for conjecture. As was often said within the Pentagon, 1 percent of the US economy paid for the long post-9/11 campaigns while 1 percent of the population fought them.

Moreover, from FDR to Reagan, strong presidential leadership has demanded a willingness not simply to reflect but shape public preferences. One of Obama's central failings has been a preoccupation with following opinion, a reflection and reinforcement of his domestic priorities and an imprudent but pervasive politicization of national security. His administration has recurrently posed a binary division between either supporting its policies or embracing an industrial strength "all war, all the time" default. But this has always been a chimera. There were, and remain, better options – especially in coercive diplomacy – to those pursued by the forty-fourth president. From Syria to China, Russia to Iran, no opponents of the president were proposing ground invasions or nation-building anew. Instead, the next administration can return to the geopolitical instincts that served America well previously: strengthening allies and proxies with men and material, utilizing US military strength and advantages in air power, special operations, human intelligence gathering, digital surveillance, space and cyber-warfare and – unless the need for armed forces is truly redundant – being willing to deploy sufficient ground troops when and where truly necessary.

Underlying all this is the urgent need to fund the armed forces properly and modernize their capabilities to confront multiple security threats and contingencies. The United States is still called upon to do more than any other nation and the optimal way to deter war remains being stronger than the rest. Washington's strategic responsibility to its allies, and its moral obligation to its armed servicemen and women, is to adequately fund the military. Asking the armed forces to protect the United States and global commons in the real world, while operating on a budget designed for one where war is receding, is as irresponsible as it is dangerous. A US foreign policy divided against itself cannot stand.

The post-Obama era

A century on from the end of World War I, humanity's capacity for self-destruction should not be underestimated. The liberal order built principally by the United States has provided unprecedented security and prosperity to billions. But it now strains under real and unrelenting pressure. The rise of non-Western states such as China, contested norms of sovereignty, and the deepening of economic and security interdependence have yielded political struggles over the distribution of roles, rights and authority within this order. Yet its internal logic remains remarkably resilient and appealing. The world America made encountered crises in the past, overcame them and evolved as a result. It can plausibly do so again.

But to avoid calamity and confirm the Obama Doctrine as a short, unhappy interlude in US grand strategy, not a blueprint for its future, requires abandoning strategic minimalism. Global challenges aplenty will remain unaddressed unless some nation or nations first direct attention to them. The strongest and wealthiest democracies bear the greatest responsibility because they possess the capacity to shape the outcomes most effectively and positively. But that requires a vision that transcends the narrowest ambitions by taking account of the greater good of the international system – not as determinative, but desirable. When a great power instead pursues its parochial interests – when it refrains from acting in the broader interest and adopts a default position of not acting at all – it betrays its responsibility. A growing number of powers can now potentially intervene to affect outcomes for good and ill. Successful management of the international system is unavoidably multilateral. But only America can act in ways that assure continued security and prosperity.

With Beijing now pursuing expansionist claims to almost the entire East China and South China Seas, only the United States can demonstrate the risks of unravelling the fragile Asian balance of power that allowed the Chinese economy to grow in the first place. With a resurgent Russia threatening a similar convulsion in Europe, only America, in tandem with its allies, can deter and contain Moscow. And only the United States can restabilize the Middle East, prevent the Saudi-Iranian cold war and its proxy offshoots from becoming hot, and preclude its descent into a region of permanently warring extremist sects and nuclear-armed states threatening the West. To those imagining otherwise, two questions need answering: If not America, who? And if not now, as the unravelling of the international system threatens to tear the liberal order asunder, when?

The United States remains both anchor and sail of the international system. But by design and execution, recent strategy has proven unfit for America's purpose. Obama's policies have appeared set upon rendering the United States a "normal" nation, unburdened by notions of a special providence or distinctive vision. Their running up against the brutal real world has left an administration in denial and America with an overall grand strategy that seems opaque when not opportunistic, and opportunistic when not opaque. Moral confusion has replaced clarity. Weakness has proven an incitement. The notion that engagement and exemplarism can transform recalcitrant adversaries into responsible partners, and that working through international institutions can preserve US influence over world affairs at reduced cost in blood and treasure, has proven a costly illusion. An unrealistic strategy has diminished America to an ad-libbing understudy on the world stage, where reactive last-minute tactics substitute for effective strategic vision.

Whether, and for how long, Americans continue to resist the siren song of neo-isolationism from right and left remains a "known unknown." Perhaps the new zenith of Washington's global ambition is one where only FIFA (the Fédération Internationale de Football Association) need fear American boots on the ground during dawn raids in the badlands of Zurich. But there is reason to believe that elegies to American power are premature. The United States can recalibrate its future, recapture its purpose and renew its promise by restoring the key features of international leadership egregiously neglected by Obama. The past can serve as prologue. Returning to the strategic offensive in a "reset" of US leadership will necessitate the unapologetic and unabashed use of all elements of national power to resurrect a genuine peace through strength: the revival of military might, economic engagement, diplomatic realism and a compelling ideological vision.

Effective prescription necessarily relies on accurate diagnosis. The pages that follow offer neither a jeremiad nor a Cassandra-like prophecy of inevitable gloom and doom. Demand for American leadership remains high; only the supply is low. In 2016, the electorate has the opportunity to turn a new page with a president whose instinct is to oppose rather than appease America's enemies and urgently repair the growing cracks in the security architecture of the Western alliance: less "yes, we can" than "yes, we must." The argument in this book rests centrally on the conviction that the United States can and should resume its mantle of global leadership, through achievable strategies at acceptable cost. The next chapter appraises the four lessons of Obama's failed record before considering the prospects for a renewal of strategy in Chapter 3. In Chapter 4, the common assertion of American decline is challenged before, in Chapter 5, a possible route to renewing US leadership is set out.

That path – let's call it a New American Internationalism – should comprise five elements:

i. *Rebuilding National Security and Defense*: urgently but steadily increasing defense spending and rebuilding an unassailable military with a decisive qualitative and quantitative edge over all its rivals, to meet current and looming threats;

ii. *Restoring Alliance Management*: reviving established alliances, investing in new ones, and solidifying commitments to forward defense;

iii. *Reenergizing Security by Freer Trade and Securitizing Energy*: advancing a free trade regime that binds the United States closer to its European and Asian allies while exploiting the US energy revolution to reinforce collective Western security;

iv. *Reviving Muscular Internationalism*: affirming deterrence and engaging in assertive counterterrorism, without ill-founded assumptions about the nature of state behavior, nation-building or the utility of international organizations such as the UN;

v. *Resuming Strategic Resolution*: substituting resolve for patience, with moral clarity on core values, to ensure the broadening and deepening of liberal international order.

The jury will remain out for some years on whether Obama will be remembered as a consequential president in substance as well as symbolism or whether his presidency will be judged more transactional than transformative. But history's verdict is unlikely to be generous to a tenure that began in hope and audacity only to end in cynicism and timidity. Few serious aspirants for the White House can responsibly endorse this undistinguished record. But more immediately and importantly, the next president will have the opportunity either to consolidate Obama's approach into the 2020s as a new consensus or strike a bold path of strategic revival. To the extent that foreign affairs shape voter choice, a litmus test confronts Americans in the most important (and expensive) global executive search: whom would the leaders in Moscow, Beijing and Tehran least want in the Oval Office? If the Democratic or Republican least favored by US adversaries is selected, then the 2016 campaign should turn on the candidate optimally equipped to serve as the "un-Obama."

On January 20, 2017, overlooking the west steps of the Capitol, the Chief Justice of the Supreme Court will administer the oath of office to the forty-fifth president of the United States. Immediately, that president will confront a more unstable, multidimensional and metastasizing national security threat matrix, from a weaker position, than that of 2009. "We are ready to lead once more," Obama proclaimed back then.[13] The next president will need to mean it.

[3]

Strategic sabbatical: lessons of Obama's failure

[handwritten: 29 NOTES p. 131]

"Without a well-articulated strategy that the public support and the world understands, America will lack the legitimacy – and ultimately the power – it needs to make the world safer than it is today.[1] So declared then senator Barack Obama in 2006. But this wise prescription went undelivered. According to Gallup, approval of President Obama's foreign affairs management never again reached the bare 50 percent achieved in May 2011 when Navy SEALs eliminated Osama bin Laden[2] By fall 2014, most Americans regarded Obama as "not tough enough" while almost half believed their nation was less important and powerful than a decade previously[3] Washington's diminishing influence contributed to a less secure international environment. Much of the Western world appeared to neither understand nor approve US strategy; the non-Western to exploit it. As Hillary Clinton reflected on the grand strategy of the administration she served as secretary of state, "Great nations need organizing principles, and 'Don't do stupid stuff' is not an organizing principle.[4]

Developing a "unified theory" of the Obama administration's approach to international affairs poses a formidable intellectual challenge. Its "team of rivals" changed regularly, with prominent figures such as Clinton, Robert Gates, David Petraeus and Chuck Hagel entering and exiting while the president relied more closely on an inner "echo chamber" of political advisors. Obama's concern for foreign policy appeared inconstant. And although some notable successes occurred – Osama bin Laden's assassination, partial normalization of relations with Cuba, the 2014 climate change accord with China, agreement of the Trans-Pacific Partnership (TPP) – these were strongly outweighed by a lengthy compendium of more consequential failures. Indeed, rarely has an administration been so widely criticized, not only by its partisan political opponents but also its own foreign policy principals.

The verdict of Leon Panetta, who served as CIA director and defense secretary, was that, "Too often in my view the president relies on the logic of a law professor rather than the passion of a leader. But, though true enough, the Obama leadership deficit was the result of more than lawyerly excess and insufficient passion. The president combined a complete lack of executive experience with total certitude in his worldview and the most centralized decision-making process since Richard Nixon. But whereas Nixon possessed substantial experience in world affairs and a realist understanding, Obama was a domestic policy president and foreign policy naïf whose statecraft proved an improvisation in reactive tactical adjustments. Even then, as David Rothkopf observed, "It is hard to think of a recent president who has grown so little in office" and whose "political and policy narcissism" has proven so "bad for America and its role in the world." The sabbatical from strategy was profoundly costly. Obama secured much of the progressive domestic agenda about which he cared most. But hoping that Washington could benignly retreat from a destabilizing order proved an unsustainable foreign policy.

Although each particular case is different, four related themes account for the administration's overall failure: the absence of a well-grounded geopolitical understanding for grand strategy; a naïve engagement approach; pervasive politicization; and overcommitting while underdelivering, through inattention to the necessary effort – at home with the Congress and American public, and abroad with key allies – that ensures genuine leadership. Cumulatively, they ceded US influence, eroded credibility and squandered opportunities to secure crucial goals. The result was that internationalism was retarded when the conditions for its strengthening appeared propitious. Pivoting to America – as emphasized by the one-quarter of 2010's National Security Strategy devoted to "nation-building at home" – negated effective engagement abroad. As one senior administration official recounted:

In the cocoon of our public debate Obama gets high marks on foreign policy ... because his policies' principal aim is not to make strategic decisions but to satisfy public opinion – he has done more of the things that people want and fewer of the things we have to do that may be unpopular. To our allies, however, our constant tactical maneuvers don't add up to a coherent strategy or a vision of global leadership. Gone is the exuberant American desire to lead in the world. In its place there is the image of a superpower tired of the world and in retreat ... That impression serves neither America's long-run interests nor stability around the world.

We cannot know whether another president would have fared better or prevented the vacuum in the global commons that has arisen. America's capacity to influence world politics has never been unlimited and it is difficult even for the most accomplished presidents to manage events. Moreover, of the multiple failures on his watch, Obama was more responsible for some than others. But in each he made things markedly worse. Had Obama not overinvested in the Iranian nuclear accord and Russian "reset," not pulled out too hastily from Iraq, not stayed aloof so long from Syria and not exhibited wishful thinking about the Afghan theater or China's intentions, some of the deployments the administration was reluctantly forced to make in its latter stages might have been unnecessary. Others could have been carried out from stronger foundations. Even then, actual commitments – to the Asian "pivot" or destroying ISIS, for instance – rarely matched stated goals. Had the imperatives of alliance management, trade promotion and communicating clearly to Americans the nature and severity of the multiple dangers facing the West been seriously attended to earlier, a more robust response to the fissiparous forces undermining global order could plausibly have been mounted. But ends and means – the core to successful strategy – were consistently out of sync.

In its latter stages, the Obama administration emphasized "strategic patience." And in an environment of diffusing power and transnational challenges, no shortcuts exist to a more stable, prosperous and just order. Many global problems have been long in gestation and pose generational tests (none more so than China, the Middle East and the Islamist threat). But under Obama, patience frequently substituted for strategy. Like the Cheshire Cat's smile, the rhetoric of engagement remained after the substance had atrophied. Meeting global challenges instead requires firmness and clarity. Most notably, where vital national interests are implicated, America must be prepared to fight: to kill and die. The Obama taboo on deploying ground forces proved self-defeating. Constructive containment and effective deterrence require strategic clarity, not ambiguity, about redlines that cannot be crossed; adequate diplomatic, economic and military responses to guarantee that the costs of aggression exceed any anticipated benefits; and unassailable credibility about the determination to fulfil stated commitments. A sound post-Obama strategy must be premised less on patience than resolve and learn the "teachable moments" of the failed Obama years.

Lesson one: the imperative of grand strategy

Although tactical errors exacerbated its implementation, the fundamental fault in the Obama Doctrine was its design.[8] The administration's strategic assumptions were ill-founded and unsafe. While some critics claim that the problem was less a bad strategy than pursuing no discernible strategy at all, Obama's policies flowed from a particular conception of the world and America's appropriate place therein. The approach proved a bold but flawed experiment, "as a prolonged counterfactual take on what the world might have been like for the last 70 years without a traditionally engaged American president dedicating our country to preserving the postwar Western-inspired global order.[9]

An optimal grand strategy – the purposive use of military, diplomatic, and economic tools of statecraft to achieve desired ends – requires realistic evaluations about Washington's "opportunity structure": the international system and America's evolving role. Cold War containment provided the template, with Democratic and Republican administrations adapting but never abandoning its central tenets. After the USSR collapsed, successive administrations charted new courses. In 1990, George H. W. Bush proclaimed a "new world order" that he did not secure reelection to manage into being. Bill Clinton ran on a campaign slogan that "it's the economy, stupid" only to see his presidency proclaiming America the "indispensable nation." George W. Bush spoke as a presidential candidate for a more "humble" approach and against nation-building but left office having spent a trillion dollars trying to accomplish precisely that in Afghanistan and Iraq. But whatever their marked differences, recalibrations and failings, presidents from 1945 to 2009 followed a bipartisan tradition.

Obama's sabbatical departed that legacy. As such, the animating impulses of Obama's statecraft were not incidental but intrinsic to his conduct of foreign relations. Central was the notion that, while circumstances differed vastly from 1991, Obama could also redeem a "peace dividend" from the aftermath of "Bush's wars." That, in turn, was based upon a conception of international relations that none of his predecessors shared – a new understanding of a world in which power was diffusing and where the salient issues were not interstate but global in nature, requiring unprecedented cooperation. But such cooperation was feasible since global public goods constituted a new form of national self-interest and could be advanced as such. "The pursuit of power," Obama declared (in Russia, ironically) "is no longer a zero-sum game."

The administration's problems thus stemmed from an overriding preoccupation with domestic policy and a profound misunderstanding of a world order in flux. Without the domestic focus, international realities might have intruded earlier. With it, and emboldened by the false certainties that globalization was redefining international politics, geoeconomics trumped geopolitics and interstate war was a relic of the past, the administration framed an approach to facilitate retrenchment and accommodate adversaries. This was premised on the notion (more prosaically, an aspiration) that those adversaries would repay accommodation and buy into the existing system through American displays of contrition, atonement and goodwill.

While Obama was right about the importance of global issues, he was emphatically wrong about power politics. Moreover, his mistaken analysis was outlined and operationalized at precisely the moment when the states whose cooperation he needed most – China and Russia – were adopting increasingly unrepentant paths of expansion and belligerence. Yet Obama, maintaining a habit of thought characteristic of intellectuals – developing universal theories and then adjusting objective reality to them, rather than the other way round – was slow to accept this. Few expected Obama to act as a foreign policy maven, an American Machiavelli or Metternich. But the president's belief in the power of moral authority, even where historical animosities and strategic divergences had calcified to the point of immutability, trumped the appropriate regard that ought to have been paid to the harsher *realpolitik* of the balance of power. Obama did display a prudential pragmatism and conservative style that comported with realist sensibilities, but in service of a naïve vision that was less strategic than conventionally ideological (idealist and cosmopolitan) in its mis-placed faith in international organizations and law.

But geopolitics never went away. Strategic polyamory – where states with supposedly malleable strategic personalities, from China to Iran, offer the United States plausible "partners" – was never viable. The end of the Cold War let the genie of coercion out of the bipolar bottle of containment, advanc-ing two major power shifts that fundamentally realigned regional orders, with consequences affecting all nation-states: a transition between states (prin-cipally from west to east) and a diffusion from states to sub- and nonstate actors. While Washington chose to regard international relations as no longer zero-sum, other states repudiated that vision. Threats to security and pros-perity multiplied both at the systemic level, where dissatisfied major powers increasingly challenged international order, and at the state and substate level, where disaffected ethnic, tribal, religious and other groups destabilized key countries and entire regions. Among disputes that have historically generated the greatest conflicts, the most dangerous to global order remain disagree-ments over the international system and major powers' prerogatives in their immediate neighborhoods – the core of US tensions with China and Russia. But the most serious to the immediate physical security of Americans are the cyber threats from Moscow and Beijing, and the nonstate Islamist groups that retain the intention, if not necessarily the capacity, to inflict catastrophic losses on the homeland. An effective strategy needed to tackle *both* sets of antagonists simultaneously.

Had Obama articulated a clear statement of retreat from this unhappy world, the American public and US allies could at least have understood what course the White House was navigating. Such a path would undoubtedly have attracted censure. But "restraint" would have had the merit of clarity as well as coherence. There has long existed a respectable and cogent (if flawed) argument – "offshore balancing" – that the United States should downsize its foreign commitments, refocus at home, and switch resources from defense to domestic discretionary spending.[10] While unwelcome, allies could at least be clear that the era of NATO as a fraternity of freeloaders was over: US security guarantees were now limited and conditional while the imperatives of greater self-reliance, increased defense spending and more proactive initiatives were the order of business.

But Obama did not choose to make such a clear break. Instead, the admin-istration remained stuck between the rock of a refusal to fully embrace the military necessities his commanders elaborated and allies desired, and the hard place of denying that retrenchment and retreat were even occurring. Obama thereby satisfied neither those maintaining the importance of a forward-leaning posture nor those seeking an unequivocal departure from the Bush era. The result was that, as one diplomat of a US ally lamented, "You're still a super-power ... but you don't know how to act like one."[11]

Lesson two: the limits of engagement

H. L. Mencken famously observed that, "For every complex problem, there is a solution that is simple, neat, and wrong." In Obama's case, ameliorating global disorder required engagement. And engagement proved mostly simple, neat and mistaken. Rarely, if ever, has US engagement yielded such widespread estrangement of allies and fortification of adversaries.

Engagement can succeed and often represents a logical and sensible choice. "Jaw, jaw," Churchill advised, is invariably preferable to "war, war." But the United States possesses a Qualitative Diplomatic Edge. Effective engagement needs to be calibrated to recognize that Washington is typically in the more advantageous position, conditionality is preferable to a "pure" policy of carrots without sticks and, when failing, the approach needs to change. Obama's statecraft instead vindicated Frederick the Great's warning that diplomacy without arms is like music without instruments. A successful strategy cannot be based on battle fatigue. Absent the credible willingness to use coercive pressure, demilitarized diplomacy relied too heavily on good faith, moral suasion and selective sanctions. Framing an entire grand strategy in these terms risked resembling more a glorified public relations device – a strategic placebo – than a closely thought-out prospectus for practical policymaking. This was especially so when, far from proactive attention and consistent focus, the administration more often appeared disengaged to, or even dismissive of, allies but so solicitous of adversaries that Washington assumed the weaker position of supplicant: Samson without his locks.

As proof of engagement's superior wisdom, Obama was apt to invoke Cold War presidents talking to the Soviets. But the president presented a rose-tinted history. Not every Cold War conflict was settled with an exchange of superpower phone calls. Even where the example of Nixon going to China offered a precedent for transformative diplomacy, it is worth recalling what happened: not a sudden transformation but the beginning of a thaw that more than forty years later remains incomplete and eminently reversible. And despite the fact that blood was shed often and aplenty, the Cold War order was, ultimately, orderly. By contrast, Obama's cosmopolitan world of legalism and accommodation foundered upon an alternative universe of nationalism and adventurism. Ethnocentrism and xenophobia, far from being Western preserves, proved powerful universals, more so than respect for international law, human rights and government based on popular consent. The notion that antipathies based on decades of conflict, divergent interests and distinct values could be resolved through dialogue – that marathons could be turned into sprints – lacked even a cursory familiarity with historical reality.

The problems with the perverse incentives of Obama's engagement calculus were well-captured by Robert Kagan, writing years before Moscow invaded Ukraine and intervened in Syria:

Experts on today's Russia argue that, notwithstanding occasional neo-imperial rhetoric, the rulers in Moscow have no desire to restore the Russian Empire, to take charge of the Baltic states of Lithuania, Latvia, and Estonia, or to reunite old Soviet republics like Ukraine, Moldova, Georgia, and Belarus. But is this because they are constrained by the global power equation from realizing these ambitions, and so temper them? There is no way to know for sure, but history suggests that when we look at the behaviour of nations and try to understand their motives and ambitions, we need to be aware that their calculations are affected by what they believe they can achieve and what they believe is off-limits.[12]

Under Obama, the zone of the achievable to American adversaries dramatically widened, while that of off-limits activity shrank. The results confirmed engagement less as strategy than hope. Three cases are especially instructive: Iran; Russia; and the rise of ISIS.

Iran

Iran was the very definition of bad policy. Moreover, because of its profoundly negative consequences for nuclear proliferation and Iranian regional hegemony, it represents the most vivid expression of flawed strategy. Obama claimed that when he entered office, "the world was divided and Iran was in the driver's seat" but that, if Tehran seized the opportunities his administration provided, it could become "a very successful regional power … abiding by international norms and international rules.[13] Instead, a brutally repressive regime facing possible collapse in 2009 was enabled by Washington to consolidate its hold on power and extend its imperial project in unprecedented ways.

Iran entered nuclear negotiations heavily sanctioned, internationally isolated, an economic basket case, and by far the weaker partner. Yet the United States made all the major concessions. The 2013 talks' premise was that Tehran would have six months in which to give up its nuclear program or face even more devastating sanctions. Having insisted on abandoning its nuclear facilities and ceasing all activities relevant to bomb-making, however, Iran was allowed to retain its nuclear infrastructure and continue some of those activities. Against UN Security Council and EU resolutions mandating an immediate stop to enriching uranium, Iran will continue to do so with less than half of its previously operational centrifuges and be allowed to resume all nuclear activities in ten to fifteen years – establishing the Islamic Republic as a "threshold" nuclear weapons state with the international community's blessing. Obama asserted in his August 5, 2015, speech at American University that the accord "permanently prohibits Iran from obtaining a nuclear weapon." But it does nothing of the sort. Rather, in every respect, Iran has been empowered.

The Joint Comprehensive Plan of Action (JCPOA) signed on July 14, 2015, "concedes an enrichment capacity that is too large; sunset clauses that are too short; a verification regime that is too leaky; and enforcement mechanisms that are too suspect.[14] Contrary to the Reagan mantra of "trust, but verify," neither trust nor verification are feasible, given the absence of "anytime, anywhere" inspections, permissive standards for data collection by Iran itself rather than the IAEA and Iran's long record of strategic recidivism. Implementing a complex arms control deal with a reliably untrustworthy adversary is inherently problematic. With a slow motion Cuban Missile Crisis meeting the Thirty Years War, Obama was convinced that he could induce a change in regime behavior. But far from modifying its aggression, Washington rewarded Tehran by enhancing its power vis-à-vis its Arab neighbors just as its hegemonic regional ambitions were at their most advanced. After the Arab Spring, Iran saw a unique opportunity to exploit a region destabilized by collapsing states and unpredictable transitions. But whereas, during the Cold War, US arms control policy was linked to Soviet behavior – deals becoming politically untenable when the latter became aggressive – the Obama administration advanced negotiations in sync with growing Iranian provocations threatening the security of US allies.

Far from being transformative diplomacy, Iran got what it wanted: the lifting of the economic sanctions. In exchange, the massive financial rewards consolidated its reach by extending its sway over Sanaa, Beirut, Damascus, Baghdad, and Gaza. It is a perverse definition of a good deal that simultaneously enriches Iran by billions of dollars in sanctions relief while hoping that this reward will magic an alteration rather than an intensification in the regime's behavior or, even less plausibly, advance regime change. The deal strengthened the theocrats and Iranian Revolutionary Guards Corps rather than the Iranian people and, thereby, intensified the regional Sunni-Shia power struggle. It confirmed that America had abandoned all hope of arresting the region's descent into sectarian upheaval, state collapse and a disequilibrium of power tilting toward Tehran. As Iran expert Ray Takeyh anticipated:

The much-discussed terms of the impending agreement with Iran thus offer the theocracy all that it wants. The accord would concede a vast enrichment capacity, as well as accepting both a heavy water plant and a well-fortified underground enrichment facility that the United States once vowed to shutter. It would permit an elaborate research and development program and would likely rely on an inspection regime that falls short of indispensable "anytime, anywhere" access. In the meantime, the sanctions architecture will be diminished, and the notion of ever "snapping back" sanctions into place once they are lifted is delusional. And because the agreement itself would be term-limited, there would be no practical limits on Iran's nuclear ambitions upon its expiration.[45]

The damage done by legitimizing the nuclear program extends far beyond Iran. If nonweapon states have the "right" to large centrifuge enrichment plants, the NPT is obsolete. The United Arab Emirates, Turkey, Jordan, Egypt, Saudi Arabia, Morocco, Tunisia and Qatar possess civilian nuclear programs. For nations threatened by a nuclear Iran, these could become weaponized. By allowing Iran to retain a large-scale enrichment capacity, the UN ceded its ability to condemn others seeking the same threshold status as a matter of "right." And when that occurs, the conditions that forestalled nuclear war between the United States and USSR will be absent. A poly-nuclear region will comprise several, not merely two, nuclear powers, with none confident that its arsenal can survive a surprise attack by an adversary. In a crisis, Middle Eastern nuclear powers will therefore have strong motives to launch preemptive strikes. The chances of nuclear war – and risk that by accident, theft or state collapse, Islamist terrorists acquire radioactive material – will increase exponentially.

The negotiations progressed in the way that they did – dooming Iran to success – because, although there existed a vast disparity in power, the Iranians were convinced that the United States was adamantly opposed to using its ultimate form: military force. With Washington seemingly needing a deal more than Tehran, Obama was unwilling to walk away from the talks, a key condition of successful diplomacy. But, as Michael Mandelbaum noted, the objection to a military attack on the grounds that it would only buy time was unpersuasive. Since the Obama administration conceded that any limits on Iran's nuclear program will expire, buying time is precisely what the administration itself was engaged in. Is medical care pointless because everyone ultimately dies?[16] The issue was always the terms of the deal.

But with Iran strengthening its ballistic air defense system by acquiring from Russia advanced S-300 missiles in 2015 (missiles that may also be transferred to Iran's proxy, Hezbollah), in the event that Iran violates the deal, any air attack on its nuclear facilities may now be prohibitive. The system, with a range of up to 124 miles and the capability to strike multiple targets simultaneously, is one of the most potent. Deployed in sufficient numbers, it would render not only an Israeli but also a US strike all but impossible, the latter requiring fifth generation stealth aircraft to be deployed in dangerous, high-risk raids. Completing the theater of the absurd, Annex III Section 10 of the agreement even obliges Western experts to offer assistance to Iran with its nuclear program to help protect it against the kinds of sabotage – such as the computer program Stuxnet – used by the United States and Israel against Iran previously. Secretary Kerry even warned Israel against an attack shortly prior to Ayatollah Khamenei promising in September 2015 that Israel would be "wiped out" within twenty-five years and Iran testing – in breach of UN sanctions – an international ballistic missile.

The administration certainly had a paramount interest in achieving its goals with Iran, since a poly-nuclear Middle East would represent a catastrophic failure of decades of US policy. But in overhyping the deal as analogous to Nixon's opening to China, it falsely implied that by treating Tehran as a fire-fighter rather than arsonist, Iran's revolutionary foreign policy could be changed or contained. With forty-two Soviet divisions lining the Sino-Soviet border, China had good reason to entertain the US shared interest in preventing Moscow's hegemony in Eurasia. No comparable common interest animated Khamenei who, following the accord, reiterated his view of the United States as the "Great Satan" while rejecting all cooperation on nonnuclear matters. Moreover, Nixon's efforts were part of the broader struggle against communism; Obama's accomplish nothing in the civilizational struggle against Islamism and may plausibly retard that effort. In Vietnam, Nixon's goal was to cease "Americanizing" the war and coerce the Vietnamese to assume its responsibility. Generalizing the policy to deputize elsewhere, Iran became the principal American proxy in the Gulf. But where the Shah's Iran was a Western-oriented, secular and pro-US power, Iran remains an anti-Western, theocratic and anti-American regime. Like its erstwhile enemies in al Qaeda and ISIS, Tehran's ultimate strategic purpose remains to oust the infidel from the region, replace US hegemony and subordinate or annihilate America's allies. By appeasing Iran, Obama not so much permitted this process of driving Washington out of the region but assumed the codriver's seat and placed his foot on the accelerator. January 16, 2016 – "Implementation Day" of the Iran deal – may yet be remembered as the inflection point in the geopolitics of the Middle East and the prelude of "Detonation Days" to come.

Russia

It has been a truism since 1991 that the United States must find a way to coexist with Russia, a great power with legitimate interests that cannot be ignored. But what matters are the terms of coexistence. Russian aspirations for an "equal partnership of unequals" have foundered on the asymmetry of the bilateral relationship. While America has been Russia's top priority, Moscow has been a second order priority for Washington. But under Obama's form of updated détente, Moscow perceived its international options to have widened. Little was off-limits to constrain its burgeoning ambitions.

In 2009, Secretary Clinton prematurely hailed the misbegotten "Russian reset" as a "win-win" proposition for Washington and Moscow. To placate Putin, the United States abandoned a missile defense system that Poland and the Czech Republic had agreed to host, concluded nuclear arms reductions in New START and cut its military presence in Europe. In return, the United States gained logistics routes to Afghanistan and limited assistance in the UN on Libya and Iran, while Russia reasserted its Middle Eastern presence more strongly than at any time since the 1970s, annexed Crimea, invaded Ukraine, provided safe haven to Edward Snowden and promulgated a new doctrine that threatened the use of tactical nuclear weapons in any conflict with NATO involving its neighbors. Facing an administration that he perceived as weak, indecisive and risk averse, Putin positioned Russia as the heir to the Russian Empire as it existed under the czars.

With war on Ukraine, the reset disintegrated and US-Russian relations deteriorated to a pre-Gorbachev era, thereby cementing a new cool, if not cold, war. While the ideological antagonism is more muted, Russia contends that its values are different from and superior to those of decadent America. Moreover, embarked on its largest military build-up since the Soviet Union collapsed, year-on-year defense spending increases are a state priority for Putin. Kremlin plans call for an increase of one-third in the numbers of active duty military personnel to 1 million by 2020. In addition to a new battle tank, the T-14

Armata – the world's most lethal – planning encompasses 1,200 new planes and helicopters, 50 new surface ships and 28 additional submarines.

Crucially, the regression in bilateral relations extended beyond the "post-Soviet space." Moscow's obstructionism and recalcitrance encompassed reneging on the 1987 Intermediate Nuclear Forces Treaty by placing battle-field ballistic missiles (previously banned under the treaty) in place, attempting a *rapprochement* with China on trade and security issues and passing punitive measures in response to US and EU sanctions. Putin's overarching aim is clear: to divide and neuter the Western alliance, fracture its collective approach to security, render NATO as threatening as the Nepal Association of Tour Operators and end America's role as a European power. His revanchism – an unsubtle mixture of subversion, threats and disinformation, while funding European parties of the far left and far right – has been unsated by the Crimea annexation and war against Ukraine.

Failure to respond to Putin's multiple provocations reinforced the many signals of US weakness. After Crimea was annexed in 2014, Obama denounced the Kremlin for "challenging truths that only a few weeks ago seemed self-evident, that in the 21st century, the borders of Europe cannot be redrawn with force, that international law matters, that peoples and nations can make their own decisions about their future." Yet even after those borders were again trans-gressed that year in Ukraine, Obama dignified US policy in his 2015 State of the Union as a triumph of "American strength and diplomacy ... We're uphold-ing the principle that bigger nations can't bully the small by opposing Russian aggression and supporting Ukraine's democracy." The credibility gap that this confirmed with a litany of unfulfilled assurances proved to be less a case of Nixonian deception than a product of wishful thinking and stubborn adher-ence to failing policies. Once it became clear that Russia was violating interna-tional agreements and Ukraine's sovereignty, Obama's "tough" response was to make plain that the United States would not respond militarily but would impose selective economic sanctions that, however painful to his gangster cabal, were manifestly insufficient to force Putin to back down. The "Minsk 2" peace plan, agreed to by Russia in February 2015, went unimplemented while Obama steadfastly refused requests by the Ukrainian government even for defensive weapons to blunt Russian attacks. In short, and neither for the first nor last time, Obama committed the United States to a battle that he had no intention of pursuing to victory.

The unilateral Russian military action in Syria represented an unprec-edented deployment in recent Russian history, deep in a Middle East from which it had essentially disappeared since 1991. With breathtaking speed and chutzpah, Moscow managed not only to establish major bases, person-nel and material but conduct regular air sorties against the anti-Assad rebel forces under the guise of attacking an ISIS terrorist threat that the United States was unable to overcome. A geopolitical challenge unlike any that US Middle East policy had faced for four decades, Moscow's gambit was a classic balance-of-power maneuver to simultaneously bolster the Shiite presence in Syria and contain the Sunni jihadist threat from reaching Russia's southern border. But it also had the happy coincidence of humiliating Washington, projecting Russia power, testing its military in combat and offering to regional actors an example of a great power able and willing to deliver on its stated commitments. As such it represented the most glaring symptom of the disintegration of the US role in stabilizing the regional order that emerged from the Arab-Israeli War of 1973.

Time and again – even when he was nominally less influential during Dmitri Medvedev's presidency from 2008 to 2012 – Putin outflanked and outmaneuvred the Obama administration: turning Syria from a candidate for potential regime change to one where Washington exhibited *de facto* support for Assad; transforming the possibility of the US arming Ukraine into a "ceasefire" perpetuating Russian control of eastern Ukraine and intimidating its western half; threatening further "hybrid warfare" in the Baltics; dividing the EU internally and against the United States; expending $400 billion on a thirty-year deal with China to insure against European reprisals on Russian energy exports to the West; and confronting a "twenty-first century" postmodern EU with the crudest of nineteenth-century economic and security threats while posing as the stabilizing force in Syria that would stem Europe's refugee crisis, whose divisive effects it sought to exploit.

A half-century on from their dramatic rift, Russia's relations with China are also restabilizing on the basis of a Russian pivot to Asia. On the basis of shared mistrust of US power, a common embrace of a multipolar order predicated on absolute national sovereignty (Ukraine notwithstanding), and a growing trade and arms relationship, Beijing and Moscow share a vested interest in exploiting Western weakness and wishful thinking. By reviving fears over European security, challenging NATO's integrity, impeding the American pivot to Asia and stretching strained resources, Russia's contemptuous rejection of Obama's outreach has contributed powerfully to the erosion of US leadership and global order. But throughout, America has – even in the case of a Ukraine whose leaders see themselves as fighting in defense of Western democracy against imperialist autocracy – been otherwise "engaged." Where George Kennan once produced a blueprint for standing up to the Soviet Union without starting a war, Obama produced a blueprint for accommodating Russia in order to avoid war, no matter how severe the geopolitical costs. The beginning of strategic wisdom is to treat Russia not as a pariah state but one whose trajectory is more likely to prove either confrontational or chaotic than cooperative, and to prepare the US military and bolster deterrence accordingly for Moscow's future power projection and continued pursuit of conquest by stealth.

Iraq, Syria and the rise of ISIS
The flip side to the mistaken overinvestment in Iran and Russia was the underinvestment in key security challenges in the Middle East, where a dangerous

disengagement compounded the loss of credibility and influence, fueled chaos and the collapse of the region's geopolitical framework and hastened US retreat. The priority accorded the Iranian deal and mismanagement of relations with Israel, Egypt and Saudi Arabia convinced friends and foes alike of Washington's exit as the regional hegemon. But most of the administration's errors were unforced and entirely of its own making.

In Iraq, Obama lost victory by prematurely calling an end to war while failing to win the peace. When the United States toppled Saddam's regime in 2003 and mismanaged securing the nation, two decades of suppressed sectarian feuds were unleashed in a Hobbesian free-for-all. But with the success of the 2007–08 surge and Anbar Awakening, US forces had established the conditions for moving forward with state-building. Vice President Biden even expressed his optimism in 2010 that Iraq would become "one of the great achievements of this administration." The president confirmed as much when he welcomed returning troops at Fort Bragg by declaring on December 14, 2011, that "we're leaving behind a sovereign, stable and self-reliant Iraq" at a "moment of success." Although the Status of Forces Agreement concluding the US presence in 2011 had been negotiated by the Bush administration, it is unlikely that Bush would have left without a residual force presence in the conditions that then obtained.

But the Obama administration had no appetite to stay the course. Rather than maintain a US presence as an insurance policy as the military advised, its sole imperative to end "Bush's war" authored crucial errors: ignoring military recommendations for the number of troops needed to train Iraqi forces and maintain stability; overlooking Nuri al-Maliki's autocratic and sectarian behavior as prime minister; minimizing Tehran's malign intervention; and siding with Maliki's State of Law coalition over the nonsectarian Iraqi National Movement that won two more seats in the March 2010 elections. Together, the decisions cemented institutional sectarianism, lost intelligence networks painstakingly established over several years, and weakened the Iraqi and US responses to the rise of ISIS.[17] By October 2015, the Iraqis were establishing joint intelligence networks with Iran, Russia and Syria and inviting Russian air attacks on ISIS in their own territory.

In Libya, in a concession to advocates of humanitarian intervention, on March 19, 2011, Obama unilaterally authorized "a limited military action" to protect civilians threatened by Colonel Qaddafi. Intervening was "in the interests of the United States and the world" and six months later, in a September 21 speech to the UN, the president declared:

Forty-two years of tyranny was ended in six months. From Tripoli to Misrata to Benghazi, today Libya is free ... Yesterday, the leaders of a new Libya took their rightful place beside us, and this week, the US is reopening our embassy in Tripoli. This is how the international community is supposed to work: nations standing together for the sake of peace and security, and individuals claiming their rights.[18]

Thereafter, lacking US follow-up, the embassy closed, four Americans were killed in Benghazi, the state collapsed, civil war engulfed the nation, a refugee crisis was created, and a new haven for ISIS developed directly facing Europe's southern shores. Libya represents a chaotic failed state threatening indefinitely to destabilize North Africa.

The refusal to stay the course in Iraq and botched Libyan intervention informed the reluctance to intervene in Syria. Official policy shifted erratically from a rapprochement with Assad, whom Hillary Clinton in 2011 had termed a "reformer" (after the administration restored diplomatic relations severed by Bush following the assassination of Lebanese Prime Minister Rafik Hariri) through mild support for democratizing forces to concern over the destabilizing consequences of Assad's overthrow. With the regime engaged in industrial strength murder of its citizens, Washington eventually issued statements that Assad "must" go. But failure to enforce the publicly stated "redline" on this and the use of chemical weapons shattered what slim credibility remained. The result was to harden Assad's resolve.

As civil war intensified in 2012, Clinton and then-CIA director Petraeus developed a plan to vet Syrian rebels and train a cadre of fighters whom the United States would supply with weapons. But, though supported by Panetta and Joint Chiefs of Staff Chairman Martin Dempsey, the plan was vetoed by the president. A successful regime change in Syria to a responsible post-Assad government could have yielded substantial strategic gains: the end of Iran's sole Arab ally; termination of supply lines to Hezbollah in Lebanon; an increase in Israel's security; and limiting Syrian destabilization of Iraq. Instead, Syria policy became another exercise in indecision and disarray. Prizing the Iranian deal above all else and fearing Russian disfavor, Washington managed to alienate its Sunni allies while making clear to Tehran, Moscow and Beijing its losing hand and that the days of US coercive diplomacy were numbered.

Along with the abandonment of long-term ally Hosni Mubarak in Egypt, the failure to enforce the Syrian redlines cannot be underestimated. It damaged Obama and diminished US standing. Exactly how much the decision reflected geopolitical or electoral considerations remains unclear. But whatever the motivation, the result was a pellucid signal to adversaries within and outside the region that Washington was at best indecisive, at worst paralyzed and profoundly averse to deploying serious military force. The president showed no inclination to get involved, despite a mounting death toll estimated at roughly a quarter of a million Syrian lives lost, 4 million refugees and 8 million more displaced. Yet the humanitarian and geopolitical catastrophe ultimately dragged the United States into the conflict anyway.

It is impossible to know if the Petraeus plan would have succeeded. But what we do know is that a minimalist approach wasted valuable time and sacrificed influence on the ground. Without US support, moderate rebels could neither defeat Assad nor keep more extreme elements at bay. That allowed ISIS to capture much of eastern Syria and, in 2014, to sweep across northern and western Iraq, take Mosul and declare a caliphate. Ultimately the United States intervened with air strikes, training and arming moderate Syrians while the Saudis, Turkey and UAE ignored administration objections to train and supply more extreme anti-Assad groups. In Syria, where the regime confronted a range of secular, religious and Salafist forces, along with ISIS, the United States proved unable to meld the factionalized non-ISIS groups into a strategically effective force. Moreover, the United States could neither make its peace with the Assad/Iranian regime because of its repressive policies, nor defeat ISIS with the inadequate forces deployed.

The emerging fight against ISIS changed the narrative but not the substance of Obama policy, as the United States returned to war in Iraq. But the delay in action allowed ISIS to build up its money, capability, strength and weapons in Syria and facilitated its move into Iraq. Ceding influence to Iran ensured that many Iraqi Sunnis refused to take up arms against the jihadists. Despite warnings from his intelligence agencies, Obama failed to take ISIS seriously, which he ridiculed as a "jayvee" (junior varsity) team in 2014. But ISIS – operating the kind of centralized command and control that makes it far more effective than prior nonstate forces – went on to control a volume of resources and territory unmatched in the history of extremist organizations. In Iraq, there were insufficient ground forces to make them effective, rendering US "Operation Inherent Resolve" more akin to "Operation Whack-a-Mole." While ISIS experienced territorial setbacks, the jihadists spread their influence and membership from Libya and Tunisia to Afghanistan. On September 4, 2014, Obama stated publicly that, "We don't have a strategy yet." Nine months later, at the G7 meeting in Germany, he conceded that the United States still lacked a "complete strategy" for training Iraqi forces to combat ISIS. Yet more foreign fighters had traveled to Syria and Iraq to join ISIS than went to Afghanistan to fight the Soviets in the 1980s. By the summer of 2015, ISIS controlled up to one half of Syrian territory and one-third of Iraq.

The administration's strategic disarray encouraged freelancing by its supposed allies. The priority accorded the Iranian deal, support for Mubarak's overthrow and acceptance of his Muslim Brotherhood successor, Muhammad Morsi, and failure to enforce the Syrian redlines confirmed Washington's unreliability. This in turn led Saudi Arabia to ignore US preferences on the Syrian opposition, begin its own campaign in Yemen and (like Egypt and Syria) reach out to Russia. At the same time, the substantial capital invested by Obama in Turkey's president Erdogan yielded no consequential benefits. As its domestic arrangements became increasingly authoritarian, so Ankara became ever less reliable in its external relations. And of all its close allies, Israel's strategic position was substantially worsened by the rise of Islamist enemies on all fronts – an outcome that rendered any prospect of "peace" with the Palestinians even more distant than it had been during the administration's poorly judged attempts to mediate in Obama's first term.

The regional order sustained by the United States rapidly eroded in tandem with the collapse of central state authority. The turmoil may plausibly last a generation and no external power can restore order. But it remains in America's interest, and within its power, to contain the damage and shape a more preferable set of outcomes. Washington cannot fix the region's maladies alone. But deliberate neglect – allowing the warring forces to war – risks worsening them calamitously. When Kissinger was asked whom the United States favored in the Iran-Iraq War, he reputedly replied that it was a pity that both couldn't lose. By contrast, the Obama administration's approach permitted Iran and ISIS to advance simultaneously. While Iranian regional dominance grew, ISIS achieved the outcome that al Qaeda wanted in 2001, with movements capable of sustained combat in other Islamic countries and fanatics scattered across the West from Sydney to San Bernadino. Jihadists today control more territory than they did at the time of Osama bin Laden's killing in May 2011, rendering even the latter an increasingly pyrrhic victory for an Obama administration unable to destroy the greatest recruiting tool that Islamists have yet managed to create: a nascent caliphate in the heart of a "post-American" Middle East.[19]

Lesson three: the perils of politicization

Foreign policy is never immune from politics nor exempt from instrumental as well as principled opposition. Grand strategy has long been shaped by such conflict. Since Teddy Roosevelt, inter- and intraparty differences among Republicans and Democrats have ensured that presidents of both parties faced political opposition on Capitol Hill. But rarely has Washington seen such a pervasive politicization in which crucial matters from defense budgets to deployment deadlines have been subject to electoral and partisan imperatives, with national security deprioritized below the higher cause of a contentious domestic agenda. Although Obama shared ample blame with Republicans for the broader dysfunction, as commander in chief he bore particular responsibility for key aspects.

Defense policy
National security is not a luxury good but a constitutional duty of the federal government and a president's highest responsibility; fully funding it should be a priority. But the Obama administration's complacency about world order abetted the Pentagon's egregious politicization. The percentage of GDP spent on defense dropped from 4.6 in 2013 to 3.9 in 2015 and is on target to 2.9 by 2017. The Budget Control Act of 2011 imposed half of its mandated sequestration cuts on the military, whose share of the budget fell sharply while entitlement growth surged. In fiscal year 2014, defense accounted for 17 percent of the budget. By 2019, that will fall to 12.2 percent, according to White House projections. By comparison, defense accounted for 27 percent in 1988; in the 1950s and 1960s, the figure ranged from 40 to 60 percent.

But even these allocations belie the disturbing decline in defense capabilities. The reach of US forces is more limited, though their commitments are more stretched. As a matter of deliberate strategy, not cost-cutting, official policy calls for a smaller standing army, a dangerous approach that risks the United States being unable to mount future large-scale missions, whether in contingencies involving Russian aggression against the Baltics, conflict between the Koreas or in cases of relief operations or counterinsurgencies. As Michael O'Hanlon of the center-left Brookings Institution observed:

It is one thing for President Obama to try to avoid more Mideast quagmires on his watch. It is quite another to direct the Army not to be ready for the plausible range of missions that history, as well as ongoing trends in demographics and technology and global politics, counsels us to anticipate. In our future defense planning, we should remember the old Bolshevik saw: You may not have an interest in war, but war may have an interest in you.[20]

Obama's lodestar for a foreign policy president was supposedly George H. W. Bush. But where the Iraq War of 1991 was fought with more than half a million US personnel, 6 carrier groups, 11 divisions of ground forces and some 116,000 air sorties, today's armed forces would be incapable of mounting an operation of similar scale. And by 2021, nearly half of the defense budget will go not to updating weaponry but personnel compensation. In February 2015, eighty-five former government and military officials (including Bob Gates) wrote to congressional leaders that:

In the last three years, the Army's strength has been cut by nearly 100,000 soldiers. The Navy's contingency response force is at one-third the level of what it should be. Less than half of the Air Force's combat squadrons are fully ready. Approximately half the Marine Corps' non-deployed units lack sufficient personnel, equipment, and training. These are just some of the shortfalls that led the bipartisan, congressionally-mandated National Defense Panel to warn in its July 2014 report that the military's "immediate readiness" crisis will "lead to a hollow force" if sequestration takes effect in fiscal year 2016.[21]

Rebuilding the ship of state is prudently achieved before, rather than during, the storm. But thirty years on, the United States is still indebted to Reagan era investments. From M1 tanks and F-16 fighters to Los Angeles-class submarines, ageing weaponry stocks rely on periodic upgrades to remain operational. Command of the global commons is secure neither in the air nor at sea. Whereas, at the Cold War's conclusion, the Air Force comprised over 4,000 fighter jets, by 2014 this had declined to 2,000, with tactical aircraft squadrons down from 133 to 26 and the specialist bomber wing diminished by more than 50 percent. By 2015, the USAF possessed 158 bombers, including decades-old B-52s, B-1s and stealth B-2s (with only six B-2s available on a daily operational basis).[22] By 2009, America's naval fleet was half the size of the 600 ships of the 1980s, with planning assuming a 220-ship navy by 2030 – comprising a reduced aircraft carrier fleet of 7 or 8 (entailing only 4 or 5 deployable globally). A commitment of two or three aircraft carriers to a single emergency would become highly problematic.

The president's defenders pointed to the use of Unmanned Aerial Vehicles (UAVs) to indicate his comfort with military force. But the growing use of drones offered a strikingly apt metaphor for Obama's foreign policy: imperfect instruments, symbolic of an ever-shrinking presence, employed principally for their cheapness. The rise of drones ensured that the taxpayer costs of military action were relatively modest and manageable – $8.5 million a day, compared with $720 million per day at the Iraq War's height – and unaccompanied by US military casualties. But while using drones involves state killing, it represents war "only in the sense that buying a chocolate bar or a private jet can both be called shopping.[23] Moreover, as conflict escalates in Iraq, Syria, Ukraine and elsewhere, that cost will rise. And the more fundamental reality remains: the qualitative and quantitative superiority of the US military is suffering erosion. Such decline matters, not only for obvious contingencies such as Russia and China, but also lesser but nontrivial eventualities, from North Korean aggression to the defense of a besieged Israel to regime collapse in Egypt, Saudi Arabia or Pakistan. With an army on track to pre-World War II levels, a navy at pre-World War I levels and the smallest and oldest air force in its modern history, the United States is spending $650 billion annually on a defense budget but cannot even be sure of prevailing in a conventional war against Russia.

Undeclaring war

If funding defense was problematic, so too was the president's uncertain prosecution of the wars for which he was constitutionally responsible. Obama invariably reached for short-term political solutions to military problems. In Iraq, eagerness to exit trumped concern for what was left behind. In Afghanistan, the president split the difference in troop building requests and imposed an artificial exit date. In Mesopotamia, the stated goal was to degrade and destroy ISIS, but the president's animating desire was to vindicate his pledge to end the Iraq War and achieve his "legacy" of peace. In no instance was the US strategic interest paramount.

In some respects, though, these were mere symptoms of a more fundamental failure to explain the nature of the underlying conflict. That the US president should be meticulous in his choice of language is entirely right. But Obama's accommodationist lexicon – the refusal to use the term "Islam" or "Muslim" in conjunction with terror committed in the name of religion, the reluctance even to refer to "terrorists" – contributed to Americans turning a deaf ear to their commander in chief, while gaining nothing among Muslims at large. It ensured that by 2015–16, terrorism had returned as a major public concern and Republicans were viewed as the better party to tackle it. Much as Vietnam was at its core an intra-Vietnamese struggle, the war against ISIS represents in part an intra-Islamic conflict: an intracivilizational clash. But unlike the former, an ISIS victory is of profound strategic consequence. Nor is it one that, with some earnest talking to terrorists, promises détente with the West on the basis of shared values and mutual interest. The United States has a big dog in this fight, barking loudly and insistently. The question is less whether the fight is worth having but more how it is best won.

Answering that, however, required a broader elucidation of the stakes involved in the wider war. As the wars of twentieth century against Nazi, fascist and communist barbarisms should have taught, ideologies are harder to exterminate than individual fanatics. Both require unapologetic confrontation from without and within. Yet, of all world leaders to join directly the battle of ideas, it was not the US president but an Arab authoritarian who showed the courage and conviction. On New Year's Day 2015, President al-Sisi of Egypt made a remarkable speech in which he asked how belief in Islam had made Muslims a "source of anxiety, danger, killing and destruction": "Is it possible that 1.6 billion people should want to kill the rest of the world's inhabitants – that is seven billion – so that they themselves may live?" In contrast to Western confusion, Sisi offered a clear understanding of the dilemma posed by the Islamist menace: Islam and the Koran have two faces, one benign and one violent. Denying that religion was involved or that the violence that ISIS inflicts on non-Muslims is Koranic was part of the problem, not the solution. Muslim killers are not replacing, but offering a radical interpretation of, Islam.

As Sisi understood but Obama did not, clear and candid presidential communication is essential to prevailing against enemies who mean what they say about the destruction of Western ways of life. As both a political and spiritual force, Islam makes no distinction between the two in the way of Judaeo-Christian culture. At its core is an element of political totalitarianism dividing the world into warring halves: the Muslim ("Dar al-Islam") and the rest ("Dar al-Harb," "abode of war") with which it is in perpetual struggle, until "All religion belongs to Allah" (Koran 8:39). Might the succession of attacks by Islamists from Paris to Fort Hood, Sanaa to San Bernadino, have made more sense to Americans with more presidential candor about this animating worldview? When the president, and senior members of his administration who were in the city, inexplicably declined to attend the Paris solidarity march against Islamic radicalism after the January 2015 *Charlie Hebdo* killings, and his White House spokesperson refused to acknowledge that the Parisian delicatessen victims were targeted as Jews but "because of where they randomly happened to be," what inferences were observers to draw? Of all people, the US president should not succumb to fearing the false charge of "Islamophobia" (too often a ruse to prevent candid discussion) in place of waging the defense of civilization against poisonous threats to freedom that are anything but random.

Yet absence of clarity on the conflict was accompanied by "engagement" that abetted rather than confronted the "delegitimization" of a strong ally. Even if one agreed with Obama's high-profile outreach to the Islamic world, any rational attempt to bring about a settlement between Israel and the

Palestinians should have featured a parallel outreach to Israelis. The obverse of kindling Arab ambitions was negating Israeli fears. Yet a curiously persistent feature of Obama's engagement was his distance from Israel. As the Arab uprisings confirmed, the Israel-Palestine conflict was never central to the region's geopolitics. Among US regional priorities, the issue is one among several (Iraq, Syria, Afghanistan, containing Iran, the Iranian nuclear deal, the spread of extremism, the Yemen crisis, the Libyan implosion, Egyptian stability and reversing the eroding support among Arab allies). But the behavior and policies of the administration – from describing the Israeli prime minister as "chicken-shit" to petulant exchanges more suited to the schoolyard than statecraft – alienated Israelis when trust was critical to taking risks with their fragile national security.

The ideological and strategic groundwork laid by Harry Truman for decades of Cold War containment was consolidated by his successor, despite Dwight Eisenhower's caustic campaign criticisms of his predecessor. Unfortunately, the comparable groundwork laid by George W. Bush for the generational conflict with Islamism went unconsolidated by Obama. The next president should recognize that those who kill in Islam's name are not mere "violent extremists" but fanatics driven by a specific religion's zeal.

Lesson four: overcommitting and underdelivering

Ultimately, the preceding three lessons reflect and reinforce the defining feature of the Obama era: errant leadership. Part of the president's burden is advancing a compelling narrative. Educating and shaping domestic and international opinion matters, even if the benefits are neither immediate nor obvious. In his final foreign policy address, Bill Clinton remarked that, "People say I'm a pretty good talker, but I still don't think I've persuaded the American people by big majorities that you really ought to care a lot about foreign policy, about our relationship to the rest of the world, about what we're doing.[24] In less benign times, Obama neglected the art of persuasion. And though the administration ultimately pursued trade deals in Europe and Asia – the Transatlantic Trade and Investment Partnership (TTIP) and TPP, respectively – he invested nowhere near the energy that Clinton had to articulate the cardinal importance of free trade to US security and global prosperity.

Even in the knowledge that they are at the mercy of events and their pronouncements often entail making platitudes sound profound, presidential candidates are apt to make promises they subsequently regret. Campaign exigencies demand poetry over prose. But few figures raised expectations so high only to fail so spectacularly to deliver as Obama. As Ian Bremmer observed, "no chief executive in decades has so evidently lacked a clear foreign policy focus."[25] Although Obama frequently resorted to soaring, self-serving rhetoric, the grandiosity of the affirmations was belied by administration incrementalism. Obama heightened hopes for global cooperation while actively encouraging the diminution of the US presence and influence on which such cooperation depended. With the most powerful armed forces in the world at his disposal, the president employed military power minimally and, unlike his predecessors, was markedly unwilling to face down other states. The administration's default position was evasive action in support of the figment of a strategy. As a result, American public opinion was unprepared for the dimensions of the global challenges confronting the West.

The most consequential long-term expression of the Obama Doctrine – the imposition of stringent limits on the exercise of American power – was China. A key administration objective was upgrading Asia to the center of grand strategy: the notion that US foreign policy was overbalanced toward Europe and the Middle East and should refocus on the world's most dynamic region. An idea that animated Clinton when he assumed office in 1993 and Bush in 2001, the policy has proven difficult to implement for all three administrations due to unexpected crises (the 1990s Balkan Wars, 9/11, Russia's Ukraine War and the emergence of ISIS). The rebalance nonetheless represented the "big-picture" realist emphasis on US interests and global power shifts that marked Obama's efforts to reestablish a George H. W. Bush-style foreign policy.

But once again, in neither design nor execution did Obama succeed. Europeans, Israelis and Arabs correctly interpreted the "pivot" as a downgrading of their own regions. America's Asian allies, for whom not being forced to choose between the United States and China remains critical, were unconvinced of the seriousness of a new US approach whose principal innovation appeared to be the modest deployment of 2,500 Marines to Australia. At the same time China, though wary of a nascent containment, perceived the United States as a wounded lion, unable and unwilling to lay claim to global hegemony and ducking its traditional responsibilities. Chinese assertion in the South China Sea, turning underwater rocks into airfields to claim the rights of sovereignty and expand its air and maritime borders, met with minimal US pushback until late 2015. Beijing's provocations grew accordingly brazen, not only in its regional dimension but also in the scale and severity of cyber-attacks on the American public and private sectors.

China's ambitions to replace the United States as the global superpower also encompassed an increasing willingness to leverage its formidable economic heft. Even here, in the nonmilitary realm that is supposedly the distinctive instrument of "smart power," American suasion was insufficient to frustrate the establishment of China's Asian Infrastructure Investment Bank. The United States could have welcomed the institution and asked to play a role in shaping its norms and arrangements. By lobbying vigorously against it – only to see fifty-seven countries sign up as founding members, including close allies such as the UK – the United States inflated the Bank's strategic significance, underscored the fraying of Western ties and compounded its Asian allies' apprehensions that Washington seeks to thwart China's continued economic rise. Year 2015 may yet be remembered as the moment the United States lost its role as the underwriter of the global economic system. There have been periods of frustration before when Washington's behavior was hardly multilateral (such as the 1971 Nixon shock ending the convertibility of the dollar into gold). But it is difficult to recall any event since Bretton Woods comparable to the combination of China's effort to establish a major new institutional architecture and the US failure to persuade dozens of its traditional allies to stay out.

Against the majority of congressional Democrats and with the support of most Republicans, Obama was belatedly granted trade promotion authority in June 2015. Should Congress approve the TPP in 2016 and the United States successfully conclude negotiations on TTIP, it would go some way to countering perceptions that Washington is ill-equipped to conduct geoeconomic statecraft. But as with so much of Obama's foreign policy, much damage has already been done that may prove unrecoverable. Like Iran and Russia, China has rightly interpreted American statecraft as unusually permissive and advanced its ambitions accordingly. Only the caution inherent in Chinese strategic culture, not apprehension about US responses, has constrained Beijing from even more aggressive behavior.

Conclusion

When Obama affirmed in *The Audacity of Hope* the need for a foreign policy that Americans supported and the world understood, he conceded that, "I don't presume to have this grand strategy in my hip pocket." The profound and lasting regret is that neither did he acquire it as president. William Butler Yeats' "Second Coming" anticipated the age of Obama:

> Things fall apart; the center cannot hold;
> Mere anarchy is loosed upon the world,
> The blood-dimmed tide is loosed, and everywhere
> The ceremony of innocence is drowned;
> The best lack all conviction, while the worst
> Are full of passionate intensity.[26]

Anarchy is not necessarily chaotic. But when the center fails to hold owing to failures of conviction, things really can fall apart and tides become tragically blood-dimmed. In 2014 alone, 180,000 people were killed in internal conflicts, 3.5 more times the number than in 2010. More than 32,000 people died from terrorism in 2014. The UNHRC estimated that approximately 60 million people were either refugees or internally displaced because of conflict and violence, the highest level since World War II, equating to 1 percent of the world's population. In Syria, of 23 million people, 11 million have been murdered, displaced or fled. The global economic impact of security spending, interpersonal violence, civil conflict and terrorism in 2014 was $14.3 trillion, or 13.4 percent of world GDP – equivalent to the combined economies of Brazil, Canada, France, Germany, Spain and the United Kingdom, and an increase of 15.3 percent from 2008.[27] An arc of instability, not justice, has been the principal geopolitical development of the Obama era, stretching from the South China Sea to the Mediterranean Ocean.

The Obama experiment confirms that, much as many within and outside the US wish otherwise, the world still relies on Washington. Moreover, America's enlightened self-interest is poorly served by the strategic malpractice of "leading from behind." Undoubtedly, diplomacy ought always to be the first resort in strategy, military force the last. But neither conceptually nor practically has the Obama administration overseen a coherent response to global disorder. Policies from the post-Qaddafi disengagement from Libya, nuclear capitulation to Iran and rapprochement with an unreformed Cuba exhibited an overarching emphasis on a politicized pragmatism. As a contrast to doctrinaire strategizing, that may satisfy some. But *Obamapolitik* resembled less a measured approach than an inchoate mixture of crisis management, gunboat diplomacy and *ad hoc* firefighting. The administration amassed more than its fair share of "stupid stuff." The Libyan intervention left civil war and a new terror crucible in its wake. The Iran deal was arguably the worst in US diplomatic history. Not even requiring modest alleviation of the Castros' repression in exchange for the political and economic bailout of a failing regime represented a shameful missed opportunity. Core objectives – counterterrorism, nonproliferation, energy security – were undermined by the determination to eschew the Middle East and Europe while mismanaging the prioritizing of Asia. Never before has America adopted a strategy so reliant upon constant improvisation, so negatively defined by what it cannot accomplish and so eager to make maximal concessions for minimal rewards.

Reasonable people might nonetheless prefer "prudence chic" to its more radical alternative. After all, Russia and China face serious internal pressures. Beijing's need for cheap oil conflicts with that of Moscow and Tehran for higher prices. US energy needs are less reliant on foreign suppliers than at any time since 1945. And, as Obama's Middle East adviser, Philip Gordon, plaintively observed: "We intervened in Iraq and sent troops and that didn't work out too well. We intervened in Libya and didn't send troops and that didn't work. In Syria we stayed out and that hasn't worked either."[28] But while attention to unintended consequences is invariably wise, justifying persistent inaction by being careful for what one wishes represents a nihilistic counsel of despair. The overlapping problems of containing China's rise and Russia's revanchism, combating Iranian expansion, prevailing against networked Islamist terror, preventing nuclear proliferation, maintaining freedom of the seas and safeguarding human rights together comprise the generational challenge facing the West. Progress in one dimension can all-too-easily worsen conditions in another. But simply eschewing involvement – the strategic equivalent of "Not In My Name" or "Just Say No" – offers no solution. China, Russia, Iran and North Korea will not cease playing geopolitical poker to cleave the West until their ambitious gambles are called and audacious hopes are disappointed. US adversaries need to know when aggression will meet immovable responses. Incoherent improvisation and bluffs, however centralized, deliberative and self-confident the orchestration, cannot suffice.

Despite the dereliction of strategy under Obama and the bewilderment of allies at its behavior, the United States has not been "breaking bad" on a global scale. Mature strategic personalities such as America's do not transform overnight. Washington has neither become an irrelevance nor lost the art of acting as a great power. The international order is changing and although the United States no longer dominates world affairs as it did in the 1990s, it remains preeminent. Only the United States can project power worldwide and demand for its leadership remains relatively inelastic. America cannot exercise control. No power can do so. But Washington still possesses the power to frame the choices and shape the decisions facing other states that can either buttress or disturb world order.

As such, America itself faces profound choices. The decisions voters and policymakers take now will determine, and hence must be guided partly by, where the United States wishes to be by the middle of the twenty-first century. America has been shaped by war and trade. From 1941 to 2009, Washington risked war to prevent great powers from dominating the world's economic and industrial heartlands and thereby gaining veto power over America's ability to conduct international commerce. The Obama years have called that tradition into question. But it urgently merits restoration. As Hank Paulson argues, "The simple truth is we will deal most effectively with China – and other nations – from strength, not weakness."[29] Even now, that should not be too difficult a case to make, not least when the strongest allies in the argument are Vladimir Putin, Xi Jinping, Kim Jong-Un, Ayatollah Khamenei and Abu Bakr al-Baghdadi.

As university professors know all too well, one of the few reliable social science laws is that all sabbaticals end. After Obama departs the White House, the hard work of overcoming posttraumatic strategic disorder and reviving US leadership must commence anew. Economic determinists may object but, ultimately, this is as much a matter of will as wallet. The recovery of the Western geopolitical compass – a shared sense of strategic direction and moral conviction – represents the necessary starting point to recovering the legitimacy and power to make the world safer for democracies once more.

3

"45": prospects for renewal

43 NOTES p. 133

Two objections are typically raised to the case for the next administration advancing beyond the Obama Doctrine. Both are serious and widely supported among scholars of US foreign policy and international relations, meriting direct and full discussion here.

One powerful rejoinder is that America is simply but irrevocably stuck in an inexorable decline that dates back at least to the financial crisis of 2008, the Iraq invasion of 2003 or even earlier. Realistically, no administration – Democratic or Republican – can feasibly reverse the structural atrophy of US power, even if it so desired. Nor can it hope to tame the rise of independent great powers on every continent that collectively diminish Washington's room for foreign policy maneuver. As such, arguments for reclaiming the predominant strategic culture that predated Obama are moot and, in the pejorative sense of the term, academic. Although the subject still has relatively little salience in terms of the daily preoccupations of American public life, the theme of superpower decline and concomitant notions that America's best days are behind it have often accompanied periods of internal division or introspection since the 1950s. Few commentators care to put it this way, but Obama's negative emphasis on the limits of power belied his more general embrace of a positive, "yes, we can" approach to change and progress. Or, perhaps more precisely, the self-imposed limits on America's global role were designed to facilitate the administration's progressive political, economic and social agenda at home. The costs of diminished international influence were eminently bearable. This declinist case is addressed, and respectfully challenged, in the next chapter.

A second forceful objection, distinct but related to the declinist argument, is less focused on power than purpose. On this view, there still exists either no, or at best minimal, appetite in the United States for a more assertive foreign policy. At its most elemental, neither the money nor will are there. Whatever one reckons to debates over national decline, the Obama administration and congressional Democrats won office in 2008 on a clear platform of butter over guns and faithfully reflected the insular turn in public opinion. Fatigued by failure in Iraq and Afghanistan and facing myriad problems at home after the Great Recession, Americans wanted less activism abroad. Obama was elected, and reelected in 2012, to administer a course correction to the overreach of George W. Bush's maximalist policy. And although some may contend that this turned out to be an overreaction and retrenchment went too far, it nonetheless proved preferable to seemingly perpetual war.

Tired of the rest of the world free riding on the United States underwriting global order, domestic concerns over anemic economic growth, unemployment, stagnant wages, economic inequality, crime and criminal justice, inadequate education, illegal immigration and crumbling infrastructure assumed a new prominence. And beyond these material matters, struggles over defining and redefining American identity, from race, immigration and sexuality to reproductive rights, religion and firearms, continue to preoccupy millions of progressives and traditionalists. The empirical reality is of a people continually debating America's meaning, divided between rival conceptions of the United States as an exceptional or "normal" nation, and seemingly divided on everything from abortion to Zionism. As such, a modest foreign imprint was and remains the most that Americans crave. As Obama succinctly summed up his foreign policy, "You take the victories where you can. You make things a little bit better rather than a little bit worse."

As argued previously, finding compelling evidence that things are even a little better – much less locating "victories" – is difficult. This chapter therefore appraises the prospects for a more assertive Washington after Obama. Taking account of polarized politics, presidential power and recent trends in public opinion, there is strong reason to believe that internationalism retains an appeal that is broad, deep and ripe for renewal. Although neo-isolationist and anti-interventionist sentiments command significant adherents on the right and left at a popular level, they attract minimal support among the political class or what is conventionally termed the bipartisan foreign policy "establishment." Given the intersection of these domestic influences with the contemporary geopolitical landscape of rising security threats, debate over foreign policy under the forty-fifth president is likely to be dominated less by the question of *whether* Washington needs to restore a more forward-leaning posture but *how* best to do so. History has shown that the US presidency is often defined by foreign crises. Although the raucous 2016 presidential election is likely to see sharp exchanges over the merits of the Obama Doctrine, perceived softness on national security is as unlikely to capture the presidency as perceived recklessness.

Of course, the deeply polarized character of US politics might suggest the absence of any possible consensus for moving forward post-Obama. Conflict over international affairs is built into the constitutional design and the sometimes poisonous character of recent party competition encompasses foreign as well as domestic policy. While politicians may still pay lip service to Republican Senator Arthur Vandenberg's statesmanlike admonition during the Truman presidency that "we must stop partisan politics at the water's edge," reality invariably proves otherwise. Although the budget deal struck in October 2015 was a rare and welcome instance of bipartisanship, reflexive opposition to the other party more frequently trumps policy evaluations reached on the merits and through good faith. On occasion, the parties appear not just polar but bipolar opponents. Nonetheless, although partisan polarization complicates the renewal picture somewhat, the extent to which it constrains presidential leadership on foreign and national security issues is often exaggerated. As such, *if* Obama's successor seeks to adopt an approach to foreign affairs more in keeping with the pre-2009 strategic culture, the important differences that exist between and within the two parties are unlikely to prove a decisive impediment after January 2017.

This is plausibly so even if neither party manages to win control of both ends of Pennsylvania Avenue. In part this is because, as we have seen with Obama and Bush before him, presidents retain substantial autonomy on foreign affairs. Scholars may bemoan contemporary interbranch relations for departing the constitutional equipoise established by the framers, and members of the "out-party" invariably rail against an "imperial presidency" when their particular ox is gored by the White House. But since FDR, presidents of both parties have consciously expanded presidential power. As such, the purchase of polarized politics generally has less reach on foreign and national security than domestic policy. In addition, it is worth bearing in mind that, much more so than on domestic affairs, public opinion too offers limited constraints in making choices on foreign affairs. Again, this is not to dismiss its relevance. Mass opinion does establish the range of acceptable policy options available to political leaders. But on foreign concerns, that range is normally broad and fluid. Presidents typically possess substantial latitude to forge support for their choices or even – as with Bush and the Iraq "surge" or Obama and the nuclear agreement with Iran – prevail over a hostile public and majority opposition in the Congress.

In this respect, the views of the political class and active partisans are especially important. Like publics the planet over, most Americans are too busy to acquire a forensic knowledge of global politics. Limited information provides substantial leeway to politicians to define a vision for America's world role, establish priorities and persuade the public to their side. Elite cues are crucial in informing mass opinion and shaping responses to international developments. In particular, when elites are divided, the public is likely to be as well, especially on questions of war and peace. Moreover, public opinion can be unstable and malleable in ways less true of domestic issues, even where these are controversial, such as abortion. In the summer of 2014, for example, polls indicated a popular desire to pull back from a global role and against using force in Syria. But with the rise of ISIS, headlines over the following year proclaimed majority approval for attacking the jihadists and increased support for a more assertive foreign policy.

Of course, as Yogi Berra reminded us, prediction is difficult, especially about the future. Analysts' more fevered forecasts – such as George Friedman's *The Coming War with Japan*, published in 1991[3] – can often be proven utterly wrong. Elected officials too can both surprise and be surprised. In 1980, few anticipated Ronald Reagan touring Moscow as a peacemaker seven years later. In 1992, Bill Clinton doubtless did not anticipate considering preemptive strikes on North Korea in 1994, dispatching aircraft carriers to the Taiwan Strait in 1996 or conducting an air war over Kosovo in 1999. Similarly, in 2000, George W. Bush could not have imagined launching America's longest ever war in Afghanistan. And Obama was hardly alone in being unprepared for the collapse of state authority across the Middle East after 2011. As these and other examples attest, events habitually intrude on the most well-laid strategies and plans, drastically reshaping foreign policies as much within as between presidencies.

Nonetheless, acknowledging those caveats, presidents matter immensely to the shape of grand strategy, and their approach does not simply appear from the ether as a *tabula rasa*. Moreover, there now exists a substantial literature and data on the shape of public opinion and the foreign policy divide in party politics that together form key influences on leadership. Drawing on these, the chapter advances the case for American renewal under "45" by addressing the problem of partisan polarization, the shape of public opinion and the divisions between and within the parties in the context of the admittedly highly unpredictable and convulsive 2016 presidential election. Taken together, there appears good reason to anticipate a departure from the Obama Doctrine, especially if the forty-fifth president is a Republican. But even if another Democrat reaches the White House, the post-Obama era will not require US allies to be waiting indefinitely for a more assertive Godot. The failure of Obama's strategy is likely to compel policy changes, even if these require the president to prevail over her or his fellow partisans. The Nobel Prize for Peace will probably not be returning to the White House during the next four years.

Parties, polarization and foreign policy

Historians remind us that America's international role has rarely been free from partisanship. But March 2015 saw partisan polarization over US foreign policy delve a new low. Two events signaled an unprecedented nadir between Republicans and Democrats. First, on March 3, 2015, Benjamin Netanyahu, the prime minister of Israel, addressed a joint session of Congress. Invited by the then Speaker of the House of Representatives, John Boehner (R-ILL), the White House had not even been consulted. The address offered a high-profile opportunity for Netanyahu to deliver one final scathing critique of the administration's nuclear diplomacy with Iran prior to the then deadline for the P5+1 (the Permanent Five members of the UN Security Council – the United States, United Kingdom, France, Russia and China – plus Germany) negotiations to conclude. Just two weeks before his own general election in Israel occurred – which he went on to win – Netanyahu pointedly declared that the pact being negotiated paved the way for Tehran to develop nuclear weapons, destabilize the Middle East and ultimately deliver on often declared threats to eliminate the Jewish state. Although personal relations between Obama and Netanyahu had been notoriously toxic, the origins, timing and subject of the speech made it a deeply provocative act.

Shortly thereafter, a second controversy erupted when Arkansas US senator and veteran Tom Cotton – two months into his tenure, after being elected in November 2014 – publicly issued "An Open Letter to the Leaders of the Islamic Republic of Iran" that was cosigned by forty-six Republican senators. Observing that the Iranians "may not fully understand our constitutional system," the March 9 letter noted that, "Anything not approved by Congress is a mere executive agreement" and, given the distinct term lengths of presidents and senators, most of the letter's signatories would remain in office after Obama's term-limited departure from the White House in 2017. Expressing the hope that the information would enrich Iranian knowledge of the US system and promote mutual understanding, the letter noted that, "The next president could revoke such an executive agreement with the stroke of a pen and future Congresses could modify the terms of the agreement at any time." Like the Israeli Prime Minister's address, the letter seemed expressly designed to undermine the administration's attempts to reach a deal with the Iranians over their nuclear ambitions.

Although conservatives leapt to the defense of Boehner and Cotton, many commentators saw the "hardball" tactics as definitive proof – were any still needed – that the notion that "politics stops at the water's edge" was redundant. While neither party had refused the "invitation to struggle" for the control of foreign policy that the constitution ordained by dividing authority between the presidency and Congress, the Netanyahu invite and Cotton letter together pushed partisan polarization to a new and unprecedented extreme. Never before had a Speaker invited a foreign leader – albeit of a close ally – to deliver a speech to both houses of Congress with the express intention of undermining a president's authority in ongoing negotiations with a foreign nation on an immensely important matter of national security. Nor had an exclusively partisan group of senators delivered a public letter to the leaders of another nation with the same intent (seven Republicans – including the chairman of the Senate Foreign Relations Committee, Bob Corker, R-TN – chose, for a variety of professed reasons, not to sign the letter). The March events appeared to represent more than merely the expression of sincere disagreements of principle and routine voicing of loyal opposition. Rather, they injected a divisive and bitter partisanship that had long characterized domestic politics into the heart of national security policymaking.

While the parties' distance on domestic affairs is a familiar tale that has generated extensive analysis, polarization on foreign policy is less commonly discussed but potentially no less important. Scholars and practitioners alike have identified partisanship as a hindrance to effective foreign policymaking, with the loss of a pragmatic, moderate core in both parties damaging America's capacity to have a reasoned debate about national security issues. During Obama's first term, for example, former national security adviser Zbigniew Brzezinski lamented that, "as a democracy, the US has to base its foreign policy decisions on domestic political consent ... three systemic weaknesses are complicating efforts to gain public support for a rational foreign policy attuned to the complexity of the global dilemmas facing the US": interest group lobbies, partisan polarization and public ignorance.⑤Brzezinski was only one of many convinced that the national interest suffers when foreign policy becomes partisan. And if this is the case, can we reasonably anticipate a different environment post-Obama? Does polarization imply that the renewal of US leadership depends wholly on a Republican administration after Obama? Or might it preclude even a GOP leader from developing a more assertive strategy? Surely a Democratic successor can only expect similar recalcitrance from the GOP and a Republican likewise anticipate "payback" from Democrats?

To expect otherwise would no doubt be naïve. But it is worth noting that the commonplace assertion about the evils of polarization is by no means as self-evident as Brzezinski claims. First, at a normative level, there would appear nothing amiss in a vibrant democracy for genuine disagreements over policies to occur. Neither the US Constitution nor the political system is rendered dysfunctional because there exists profound disagreement among Americans about what to do on Iran or North Korea any more than over taxes or environmental regulation. Second, many of the international matters over which there exists partisan disagreement are at least as complex as domestic issues, if not more so. Typically, the menu of feasible choices on foreign affairs comprises a series of at best unsatisfactory options. Reasonable people can and do disagree over the merits of retaliating for Chinese and Russian cyber-attacks on US public and private entities or the merits of offering lethal aid to Ukraine, as they do over reproductive rights or gun control. Third, some of the most problematic episodes in American foreign policy have historically occurred not because of deep divisions based on partisanship or principle but rather when there exists broad consensus that crosses party lines and encourages "group-think" even among America's "best and brightest" (for example, over neutrality in the 1930s, the early stages of the Vietnam War in the 1950s and 1960s and the build-up to Iraq in 2002–03).

Nonetheless, examples of sharp partisan disagreement are now disturbingly common. The 2015 conflicts over Israel and the Iran nuclear program were two recent instances. The former was only the latest expression of a growing partisan divide in which Republicans and Evangelical Christians have increasingly embraced Israel enthusiastically and unconditionally, while Democrats and

TABLE 3.1. *Wide partisan divide over Iran deal*
Among the 79% who have heard about the recent agreement
on Iran's nuclear program, % who ...

	Disapprove	Approve	DK
Total	48	38	14
18–29	39	43	18
30–49	42	41	17
50–64	54	35	11
65+	56	32	12
Post-grad	32	55	13
Coll grad	44	41	14
Some coll	48	35	17
HS or less	56	32	13
Republican	75	14	11
Democrat	25	59	16
Independent	49	36	14
Cons Rep	82	7	11
Mod/Lib Rep	58	29	13
Cons/Mod Dem	33	48	20
Lib Dem	14	74	12

Note: Survey conducted July 14–20, 2015. On the basis of those who have
heard about agreement (N = 1672).
Source: "Iran Nuclear Agreement Meets with Public Skepticism," Pew
Research Center, Washington, DC (July, 2015). www.people-press.org/2015/
07/21/iran-nuclear-agreement-meets-with-public-skepticism/

most American Jews (other than the Orthodox) have increasingly questioned
Israeli policies.[5] On Iran, in the aftermath of the July 2015 agreement, clear
and substantial partisan differences existed over its wisdom (see Table 3.1).

As the summer campaign intensified, partisanship asserted itself. In August
2015, 56 percent of Americans wanted Congress to reject the deal. Republican
opposition spiked rapidly up to 83 percent while Democratic support grew
to 70 percent. Six in ten Americans also disapproved of Obama's handling of
US-Iran relations.[6] By the following month, the week prior to forty-two Senate
Democrats sealing its fate by filibustering a procedural motion to allow a vote
on a resolution of disapproval, 49 percent of Americans disapproved the deal
while just 21 percent approved it (only 42 percent of Democrats now approved
the measure).[7]

Attempts to advance free trade agreements offer another important partisan
flashpoint, where Congress has remained reluctant to grant trade promotion
authority (TPA) to presidents – neither Bush nor Obama possessed TPA from
2007 to 2015 – never mind rapidly ratifying the results of any negotiation.[8]
Thirty-six international treaties currently remain unratified by the US Senate

thanks mainly to partisan obstruction.[9] After initially deciding to ask for congressional authority to attack Syria in 2013, Obama decided not to go ahead in the face of clear (and seemingly welcome) opposition. Republicans unsuccessfully sought a more aggressive response to Russia's invasion of Ukraine in 2014–15 in the face of a more cautious White House. And Obama's request for authorization for military force against ISIS in 2014–15 became mired in conflicts between Republicans arguing that the draft legislation was too restrictive and Democrats contending it was too permissive.

Obama himself contributed to the partisan warfare in his American University speech of August 5, 2015. Having been the object of innumerable partisan criticisms, the president countered opponents of the Iran agreement with certitude and *ad hominem* attacks, effectively declaring that no alternatives existed to his policy other than war, and that support for the deal was such an obvious call that anyone thinking otherwise had to be motivated by low politics or ideology. Noting that critics were the same people who argued for war in Iraq, the unsubtle message was that the opposition were warmongers and that in Iran, "It's those hardliners chanting 'Death to America' who have been opposed to the deal. They're making common cause with the Republican caucus."[10] From the president who once promised to transcend differences and lamented hyperpartisanship and the coarsening of national discourse, this was rather rich. As even the normally supportive *Washington Post* editorialized:

The contrast is striking between the president's tone today and his 2008 speech accepting the Democratic nomination: Looking ahead to debating his GOP opponent, Sen. John McCain (Ariz.), he pledged that "what I will not do is suggest that the senator takes his positions for political purposes, because one of the things that we have to change in our politics is the idea that people cannot disagree without challenging each other's character and each other's patriotism." There's a sad progression from that aspiration to an approach that is all about winning, even if it has to be winning ugly.[11]

Winning ugly, the Iran agreement represented the foreign policy equivalent for Obama of the Patient Protection and Affordable Care Act of 2010: a major policy achievement enacted without any support from the opposition party. Although the Iran Nuclear Agreement Review Act of 2015, requiring the president to submit the pact to Congress for review, had represented an exceptional bipartisan congressional accommodation, not one of 301 Republican lawmakers in the House and Senate – with the largest Republican majority since 1929–31 – publicly supported the actual deal. The pact represented the first US arms control agreement to be enacted with neither bipartisan support nor even a vote by both houses of Congress (Obama having forty-two Democrats in the Senate committed to filibuster any move to a vote and sustain a veto).

Such battles were unusually intense but, in one sense, familiar. No "golden age" of bipartisanship existed on foreign affairs. While the 1947–66 years are often referred to in glowing terms, even these saw significant conflict between and within the parties. From McCarthyism and the John Birch Society describing

Dwight Eisenhower as a dedicated agent of the Communist conspiracy through misleading claims about the "Missile Gap" to partisan jousting over the Bay of Pigs and JFK's fears of impeachment over the Cuban Missile Crisis, partisan conflict was constant and consequential. Even if one disregards those episodes, since at least 1966, when bipartisan agreement over containment began to fray during the Senate Foreign Relations Committee hearings into the conduct of the Vietnam War – chaired by William Fulbright (D-AK) – foreign affairs have rarely enjoyed consistent cross-party support. Carter encountered substantial Republican opposition to his Panama Canal Treaty and SALT II, Reagan faced powerful opposition to policies on arms control, Central America and South Africa, and Clinton confronted significant opposition over humanitarian intervention in Bosnia, Haiti and Kosovo, as well as the Kyoto Protocol and the International Criminal Court (signed but not ratified) and Comprehensive Test Ban treaties (rejected by the Senate in 1999). Even 9/11 ushered into being only the briefest moment of coming together between Republicans and Democrats before partisan differences resurfaced strongly from 2002. Although the build-up to the Iraq War of 2003, and its initial phase, attracted greater bipartisanship than did that of the Gulf War of 1991 – when most Democrats voted against authorizing force to oust Iraq from Kuwait – this rapidly crumbled as the underresourced occupation faltered and the central rationale for the war, weapons of mass destruction, was discredited.

Nonetheless, although the history of tribal politics in a pure two-party system is vivid, outside observers are frequently apt to question whether there exists a substantive difference between Democratic and Republican foreign policies. Non-Americans often participate in the hype of presidential elections – invariably siding with the Democratic Party candidate – only to lament subsequently the apparent policy continuity that transcends partisan differences. Indeed, one might point to certain examples during recent years as highly suggestive of the still porous character of American parties. In 2004, for example, John Kerry gave serious thought to selecting John McCain as his vice-presidential candidate, only to be rebuffed. Four years later, as the Republican nominee, McCain seriously contemplated choosing his friend and ally, former Democratic senator and 2000 Democratic vice-presidential candidate, Joseph Lieberman, as his VP in 2008, only to decide against in the face of the anticipated conservative backlash. From 2009 to 2015, Barack Obama retained a number of Bush-era GOP personnel – not least Robert Gates – and appointed other Republicans to important positions, such as Chuck Hagel as his third secretary of defense. To foreigners, polarization in American politics frequently appears a matter of the narcissism of small differences.

Some scholars lend credence to that case, arguing that comparatively modest differences of opinion obtain on foreign affairs, at least at the level of American elites. In one of the most well-known and influential, Robert Kagan advanced the case for an "Atlantic Gap" in which "Americans are from Mars, Europeans are from Venus.[12] Within the family of Western democracies, attitudes to threat perception and resolution differ because of the gulf in relative power. This predated 9/11 by many years and could be vividly seen in differences over Bosnia, Kosovo, Iraq, Iran, Russia and more. On this view, for all of the noise of partisan battles, the more prosaic reality is that relatively little separates most Democrats from most Republicans. A slightly different, and more negative, variant of this case claims that there exists a "Leadership Gap" or "disconnect" between the political class and ordinary Americans. Public majorities favor pursuing security and justice through cooperative means, prefer multilateral cooperation to unilateralism, endorse international treaties, regard securing jobs as being as important as protecting the nation from security threats and oppose actively engaging in democracy promotion – but only occasionally see these preferences reflected in Republican or Democratic administrations.[13]

But the most compelling analyses instead point to important and enduring partisan differences. Charles Kupchan and Peter Trubowitz, for example, argue that the "center" in US foreign policy has collapsed: "Democrats and Republicans remain miles apart on most matters of domestic and foreign policy, setting the stage for intractable partisanship – and wide oscillations in policy as power changes hands between Republicans and Democrats."[14] Elite partisanship is not "disconnected" from a centrist America but all too accurately reflects the views of a public that is itself divided into two antagonistic tribes over foreign as well as domestic policy. Indeed, some echo claims of an "asymmetric polarization" in domestic affairs – driven by the Republican Party's drifting further from the center to the right than the Democratic Party has shifted to the left – and claim that an intra-American "Party Gap" substantially exceeds any Atlantic or Leadership Gap:

The image of a widening gap between the dominant political ethos of Europe and of the United States misleads by misplacing the location of the true rift: the gulf does not separate the typical European from the typical American, but the modal European and many Americans from the outlook that has come to characterize US Republicans, giving them the character of outliers within the traditional community of Western democracies ... the distance separating Republicans from non-Republicans is greater than the distance separating non-Republicans from Europeans.[15]

More recently, Peter Hays Gries employed a comprehensive set of survey opinion to make a compelling case that ideological differences in mass attitudes translate into quite distinct views on foreign policy matters from China to foreign aid. Liberals and conservatives maintain consistent, but consistently different, international attitudes and policy preferences. With the exception of Israel, liberals are warmer toward all nations and international organizations than conservatives. Both ideology (widely shared and systematic beliefs about how the world works) and partisanship (the degree of party identification and loyalty) are now highly intercorrelated on foreign affairs. Moreover, even if one anticipated a policy responsive to the median voter, "The 'median voter' is less and less relevant today because the majority of House and Senate districts have become hyper-partisan."(16)

Since polarization happens at both the supply and demand ends – regardless of its origins, if no one from the other party endorses an idea, it is defined as partisan – we should expect partisan conflict to remain a constant. Separated institutions sharing powers, and possessing checks and balances on one another, preclude the type of concentrated governmental power typically seen in the Westminster model. Moreover, it is unusual to see unidirectional shifts in both the White House and Congress. But whatever the constitutional balance, the ability and will of Congress to influence foreign policy is limited in a highly partisan era, not least by the requirement for supermajorities (especially in the Senate). Even a president facing a Congress controlled by the other party needs only one-third of lawmakers in one chamber – 34 senators or 146 members of the House – to sustain a presidential veto. By acting first, presidents typically determine policy, even without bipartisan or majority support. Finally, there remain not only multiple and substantial institutional advantages to the executive on foreign affairs but also, even now, widespread deference to the White House on national security matters. A president determined to implement change – whether in a more unilateral, hard power direction, such as Bush, or in a more diplomacy-centered, soft power approach, such as Obama – can usually prevail, especially if public opinion is on side and even, on occasion, when it is not.

Public opinion: taking care of business

If the public has turned against an assertive foreign policy, then the prospects for a recovery of US global leadership would appear minimal. In America's representative democracy, elected officials are highly attentive to their constituencies, and clear opposition to an active US role would be strongly reflected in Washington. But does the evidence suggest that this is the case? Or has retrenchment under Obama consolidated a reaction that favors a less passive approach?

Certainly, if one examines opinion polls taken regularly by organizations such as the Pew Research Center, the Chicago Council on Global Affairs and Gallup, there was strong evidence for a turn away from an assertive approach during Obama's first term. The growing war weariness and focus on domestic affairs took hold during George W. Bush's second term as the United States became mired in Afghanistan and Iraq. The Great Recession exacerbated this, economic and budgetary constraints adding to the human cost of American fatalities and casualties and the financial expense of waging lengthy and seemingly unsuccessful wars. In general terms as well as on specific questions such as new armed interventions, most Americans seemed to have adopted a more insular and cautious approach.

American public opinion has long held an isolationist and anti-interventionist streak, the extent of which is heavily conditioned by international events and political leadership. Popular opposition kept the United States out of

World War II until Pearl Harbor left the nation without a choice. 9/11 occasioned intervention in Afghanistan. Absent cataclysmic events, however, appeals for "nation-building at home" invariably win support. This reached a new high under Obama. For example, a 2011 Pew poll found that 58 percent of Americans wanted the United States to "concentrate on problems at home" rather than "be active in world affairs."[17] A major 2013 opinion study by Pew found 51 percent taking the view that the United States does too much to solve world problems, while only 17 percent viewed involvement as too little. (By contrast, only 21 percent of "elite" respondents – foreign policy practitioners and experts – felt America was doing too much, while 41 percent felt it was doing too little.[18] In 2013, Pew also found 52 percent agreeing that "the US should mind its own business internationally and let other countries get along the best they can on their own."[19] ("Mind your own business" is a very American expression.)

On specific questions, too, on both Libya in 2011 and Syria in 2013, clear majorities opposed US military intervention.[20] The opposition to war even extended to retrospective evaluations of force. Over recent years, nearly six in ten Americans believed that the Iraq War was not worth fighting (though Republicans have been slightly more supportive), according to polling by the *Washington Post* and other organizations. Public opinion similarly turned against the war in Afghanistan. But any notion that Americans have embraced a new isolationism or turned pacifist is wide of the mark, for five reasons.

First, most Americans believe the United States is playing a less important and less powerful role than it was back in 2004, and that economic leadership has passed to other countries, notably China.[21] But even after "Bush's wars," Americans do not want their nation to project weakness or to be a follower in world affairs. It is especially telling that, for all their supposed war fatigue, recent years have witnessed an increase both in the proportion of Americans feeling that Obama has been insufficiently tough on foreign policy and those wanting a president who presents an image of strength to the world. Most Americans want the United States to remain the sole military superpower. Moreover, support extends for an active US role in the global economy to facilitate growth and jobs.[22] Similarly, although they have vied for top place from year to year, the public has remained wary of the same major threats to national security: Islamist terror groups, Iran, Russia, China and North Korea. Moreover, despite the controversies surrounding their use, the public gives authorities broad latitude in keeping the nation safe and employing aggressive methods against suspected terrorists, including harsh interrogation techniques and drones for extra-judicial assassinations. Only on the NSA surveillance program are public attitudes less instinctively hawkish. Americans are unconvinced by the notion that they can leave the business of the world to others without paying a significant price.

Second, Americans are not a homogeneous entity when it comes to questions of foreign entanglements or military intervention. On the latter, especially, some are *doves*, opposed to any and all use of force. Some are *hawks*, supportive of force even when this involves significant human costs. Some are *casualty-phobics* who support force as long as the associated human costs are minimal. And some (the key "swing" constituency typically determining support or opposition) are *defeat-phobics* who support the mission providing it is seen as ultimately resulting in success. As Christopher Gelpi, Peter Feaver and Jason Reifler argue, even post-Iraq, "Determined political leaders can make the use of force a credible option. Public qualms about casualties do not render the US a paper tiger."[23]

Third, "peak Obama" hit very early. Obama was never more popular than when he took the oath of office on January 20, 2009. In Gallup's first poll of presidential popularity, two-thirds of Americans approved of the job that he was doing. By July 2009, Obama was in the fifties, and thereafter he reached above 55 percent only once, shortly after the 2012 election. Despite his preoccupation with domestic matters and reluctance to risk "foreign entanglements," Obama's foreign policy approval ratings remained remarkably low. As Table 3.2 illustrates, Obama's approval ratings in his second term barely reached 40 percent on average, with slightly under two-thirds disapproving of his handling of foreign affairs. Even with major victories in his final months – in particular the mega trade deals – he is unlikely, given their controversial character, to see much bump in approval.

Over the summer of 2015, the Real Clear Politics poll average on America's direction reported a stubbornly negative spread of 30–35 percent: by September 2015, a mere 28.2 percent of Americans believed their country was moving in the "right direction" while 63 percent saw it on the "wrong track."[24] Although this owed much to domestic affairs, the drop was fueled and mirrored in assessments of foreign policy. Negative ratings helped Republicans regain the advantage that they lost to Democrats during the 2000s. A February 2015 Pew poll found 48 percent of Americans saying Republicans would do a better job making "wise decisions about foreign policy," compared with 35 percent who preferred Democrats – a 13 percentage point Republican edge, similar to the party's 10 percentage point edge before the 2003 Iraq invasion.[25]

Fourth, popular attitudes to military intervention tend to be cyclical. Support typically, and understandably, declines in the aftermath of wars, as occurred after World War I, World War II, Korea and Vietnam and, arguably, Afghanistan and Iraq. But, as those examples illustrate, declines in support hardly amount to a pacifist turn. Unlike most of Europe, there is a genuine conviction in the United States that war is sometimes necessary and just. One might even argue that, in foreign policy, the past isn't even past. For example, the debate over how to use US power that opened after the 9/11 attacks remains unresolved. In a June 2015 Gallup survey, Americans remained almost evenly divided on whether the Iraq War was a mistake: 51 percent thought that it was while 46 percent believed it was not. A clear partisan dimension informed the split. Among Democrats, 68 percent said the war was a mistake;

TABLE 3.2. *Approval/disapproval of Obama's handling of foreign affairs*
Do you approve or disapprove of the way Barack Obama is handling foreign affairs?

	% Approve	% Disapprove	% No opinion
2015 Nov. 4–8	37	59	4
2015 Aug. 5–9	39	55	6
2015 Feb. 8–11	36	59	5
2014 Nov. 6–9	31	63	6
2014 Aug. 7–10	36	58	6
2014 Jun. 5–8	32	62	6
2014 Feb. 6–9	40	50	10
2013 Nov. 7–10	39	53	8
2013 Sep. 5–8	42	54	4
2013 Aug. 7–11	40	53	7
2013 Jun. 1–4	43	52	5
2013 Feb. 7–10	46	48	6
2012 Nov. 15–18	47	46	8
2012 Nov. 3–4	49	46	5
2012 Aug. 9–12	48	45	8
2012 Feb. 2–5	48	46	6
2011 Nov. 3–6	49	44	7
2011 Aug. 11–14	42	51	6
2011 May 12–15	51	43	7
2011 Mar. 25–27	46	47	6
2011 Feb. 2–5	48	45	7
2010 Nov. 19–21	45	49	6
2010 Aug. 5–8	44	48	8
2010 Mar. 26–28	48	46	6
2010 Feb. 1–3	51	44	5
2010 Jan. 8–10	47	47	6
2009 Aug. 6–9	53	40	8
2009 Jul. 17–19	57	38	6
2009 May 29–31	59	32	8
2009 Mar 27–29	61	28	10
2009 Feb. 9–12	54	22	24

Source: Gallup. www.gallup.com/poll/1726/Presidential-Ratings-Issue-Approval.aspx

only 31 percent of Republicans did (Independents split much like the country as a whole).[26] But, amid security situations in Iraq and Afghanistan that continue to be parlous and politically contentious, a smaller share of Americans in 2015 than 2014 viewed the conflicts as mistaken. In 2015, a slim majority of 51 percent described the 2003 decision to send troops to Iraq as a mistake, down 6 percentage points from the previous year. A little more than four in 10 (42 percent) agreed that the 2001 military action in Afghanistan was a mistake, also a drop from the 49 percent reading of 2014. Democrats were somewhat less likely to see either conflict as mistaken in 2015 compared to the prior year. Looking to 2016, a *NBC News/Wall Street Journal* poll found that, for 64 percent of respondents, having backed the Iraq War either did not affect their view of a candidate or made them view the candidate *more* favorably.[27]

On more recent questions involving threats to national security and military force, there is markedly little indication of a dovish public, although there remain important partisan divides. Surveying polls from the leading organizations, it is clear that most Americans endorse using drone strikes against suspected terrorists, support air strikes against ISIS in Iraq and Syria, and do not disavow using force against Iran. Most Americans do not believe too much is being spent on national defense, do not want to dismantle US bases or disband US alliances and prefer to remain the most influential and militarily powerful nation.

The power of forgetting can also be as influential an historical force as that of remembrance. As memory of recent conflicts recedes and the reality of new challenges rises, public opinion evolves anew. Retrospective evaluations change – for example, by the summer of 2015, about as much of the population viewed George W. Bush favorably as approved of the job Obama was doing as president[28] – and mature in the face of new security threats. American opinion tends invariably to move on from prior conflicts. That, plausibly, is what has occurred over Obama's second term where, as Table 3.3 demonstrates, public opinion clearly identified the rise of serious state and nonstate threats to national security. The existence of partisan differences on some foreign policy issues should not obscure the broad concurrence on key threats, even if the question of exactly how best to deal with them is often less clear-cut.

Finally, according to Pew, by the summer of 2015, about six in ten Americans (63 percent) approved of the US military campaign against ISIS; just 26 percent disapproved. Support was somewhat higher than for Obama's first airstrikes in Iraq in August 2014 (54 percent approved). Moreover, whereas Republicans were 17 percentage points more likely than Democrats to approve military action in 2014 (71 percent vs. 54 percent), by the summer of 2015 there were virtually no partisan differences: 67 percent of Republicans approved, as did 64 percent of Democrats. But two aspects complicated this finding. First, only 30 percent of Americans agreed that the campaign was going "very" or "fairly" well. About twice as many, 62 percent, viewed it as going "not too well" or "not at all" well. Second, addressing that failure prompted disagreement. While a sizeable minority of 44 percent approved deploying ground forces against ISIS, 49 percent opposed this. The partisan divide was stark: 63 percent of Republicans favored US ground forces while an identical percentage of Democrats were against this (Independents were divided, 48 percent opposed, 44 percent in favor).[29]

In short, the notion that the Great Recession and war weariness have together tired Americans of global leadership is unsupported by the facts. According to

TABLE 3.3. *Top security threats: al Qaeda, ISIS, Iran, N. Korea*
% saying each is a "major threat" to the United States ...

November 2013	%	August 2014	%
Islamic extremist groups like al Qaeda	75	Islamic extremist groups like al Qaeda	71
Cyber-attacks from other countries	70	The Islamic militant group in Iraq and Syria, known as ISIS	67
Iran's nuclear program	68	Iran's nuclear program	59
N. Korea's nuclear program	67	N. Korea's nuclear program	57
China's emergence as a world power	54	Growing tension between Russia and its neighbors	53
Global climate change	45	The rapid spread of infectious diseases from country to country	52
Economic problems in the EU	37	China's emergence as a world power	48
Growing authoritarianism in Russia	32	Global climate change	48
		The conflict between Israelis and Palestinians	48

Note: Survey conducted August 20–24,2014. "Cyber-attacks from other countries," "Economic problems in EU" not asked in current survey.
Source: "As New Dangers Loom, More Think the U.S. Does 'Too Little' to Solve World Problems," Pew Research Center, Washington, DC (August, 2014). www.people-press.org/2014/08/28/as-new -dangers-loom-more-think-the-u-s-does-too-little-to-solve-world-problems/

the 2015 Chicago Council Survey, 64 percent of Americans wanted the United States to play an active international role, an increase of six points over the previous year. Moreover, 55 percent viewed Islamic fundamentalism as a critical threat, an increase of 15 percent from 2014 and the highest level since 2002, following the 9/11 attacks – and before the terrorist attacks occurred in Paris and San Bernadino in November and December 2015, respectively.[30] Public opinion undoubtedly remains fluid, somewhat ambivalent, and persuadable. The framing of issues and positions taken by political leaders matter in shaping public responses, as does the prospect and reality of whether or not policies succeed. But most Americans comprehend eminently well that overseas problems and dangers will not disappear through US retreat. They are not isolationists and do not want the United States to withdraw from world affairs. Rather, they desire Washington to play a responsible but leading global role: responsible in the sense of not recklessly, unilaterally without allies and partners, or blindly; and by leading, they do not mean from behind, which sounds like a euphemism for following. Most Americans do not want their nation to be the sole global cop but see clearly that it remains the only nation capable of successfully organizing collective action to tackle problems from terrorism to nuclear proliferation. They also prioritize security over privacy even as they want the latter taken seriously by elected officials.

The foundations for a renewal of US strategy are therefore strong, albeit contingent and subject to partisan pressures (with climate change and immigration by far the two most polarizing international issues in American public opinion today). A commitment to maintain a forward-leaning role rests not on idealistic, moral or humanitarian grounds, which have limited traction, but on the soundest of human fundamentals: enlightened self-interest. Americans recognize the interconnectedness of the global economy and the dark, as well as the positive, side of globalization. The ability to argue judiciously for foreign policies on the basis of linkages to domestic concerns over security, safety and prosperity is something that a president can exercise, if the political will exists and if sufficient Americans are persuaded that international matters are indeed very much part of their own business.

Foreign policy and the 2016 presidential election

Since the shape of foreign policy rests centrally on the White House, the prospects for renewing US global leadership turn heavily on the outcome of the 2016 presidential election. With no incumbent running for reelection, 2016 is an open contest and one where conditions should theoretically favor a serious Republican candidate. It has proven difficult for a party that has retained the White House for two consecutive terms to secure a third successive term (in the modern era, other than Harry Truman in 1948, only George H. W. Bush was elected to succeed two terms of a president of his own party, in 1988). With Obama's job approval ratings hovering in the mid-40s and those on foreign policy stubbornly in the 38–39 percent range over 2014–15 (where George W. Bush's had also been in his sixth and seventh years as president), profound unhappiness about the direction that America is headed, and the GOP in a stronger position in Congress and the states than at any time since the 1920s, the election should prove highly competitive.

This is not, however, to suggest that foreign affairs are necessarily likely to dominate or decide the campaign. The volatile international environment is likely to make foreign policy much more of a salient issue than it was in 2008 or 2012. Moreover, since Republicans tend to view national security and terrorism as among the most important issues, they appear to have regained some traction on these over Democrats in opinion polls (especially after the late 2015 terror attacks in France and California), and mostly view the "Obama/Clinton" record as vulnerable, the GOP will no doubt try to frame the election in large part about foreign affairs. Nonetheless, traditional "pocketbook" issues are probably at least as likely to dominate voter concerns, not least given continuing fears over the sluggish global economy, market volatility and issues from a stagnant middle class to growing inequality. In July 2015, according to Gallup, only 3 percent of Americans had listed "terrorism" and another

3 percent "foreign affairs/foreign aid/focus overseas" as the "most important problem facing this country today" (compared to 13 percent who listed "the economy in general" and another 13 percent listing "dissatisfaction with government/Congress").⑰Much will therefore depend on which party most successfully frames what the election is about.

Whether or not economic or foreign affairs dominate, what may prove at least as significant as their relative salience is that the center of gravity on foreign policy issues seems to be in a more hawkish and assertive place than that of the Obama administration. In and of itself, that represents at least a partial repudiation of Obama's record. Although the president remains very popular among Democrats and important differences distinguish the two parties, it is difficult to imagine a viable presidential contender running on an unreconstructed Obama Doctrine 2.0 platform. While not decisive, retrospective evaluations of administrations matter in elections. Few of the Obama administration's claimed achievements meet with widespread popular approval.

Naturally, it is important to be mindful that presidential campaigns are hardly a reliable site for Delphic pronouncements on international affairs. Elections are painted in primary colors. Candidates do not issue detailed plans for foreign policy, can experience campaign conversions of convenience and inflate political differences for the sake of electoral advantage. Nor is it unusual that the best-laid strategies are up-ended by events. Few analyses are therefore outside the intellectual margin of error. But appraising the state of the two parties suggests a shift away from the Obama approach. It is less the direction of change but more the question of how subtle or substantial, and how rational, sound and coherent, this promises to be.

The Republican Party

The most probable source of a shift in US foreign policy after Obama comes from the Republican Party. Reagan famously referred to the party's coalition as akin to a three-legged stool, comprising national security, libertarian and social conservatives. Although his own biography and views might have made the 2016 nomination process something of a struggle, there was no doubt that on foreign affairs the party comprised exclusively national security conservatives. Opposition to Obama's approach proved a unifying element in an otherwise fractious party and a conservative movement divided over ideas, leaders, strategies and tactics. By the first Republican presidential debate on August 6, 2015, no less than seventeen candidates had declared for the nomination: Jeb Bush, Ben Carson, Chris Christie, Ted Cruz, Carly Fiorina, Jim Gilmore, Lindsey Graham, Mike Huckabee, Bobby Jindal, John Kasich, George Pataki, Rand Paul, Rick Perry, Marco Rubio, Rick Santorum, Donald Trump and Scott Walker.

With the quixotic exception of real estate mogul and reality television star Donald J. Trump's astonishing, populist and insurgent outsider candidacy, the field was widely considered the most impressive since 1980. Comprising established and former US senators and governors, as well as notable political neophytes, it represented the four broad factions vying for influence within the party: a relatively moderate, center-right and business-oriented "establishment"; the Christian right and evangelicals; the Tea Party and populist bloc; and libertarians. But of the entire complement of aspirant GOP presidents, only Trump and Rand Paul could be considered somewhat heretical in the national security ferment. Although he adopted a more modified version of the neo-isolationism and anti-interventionism of his father, Ron, who had run unsuccessfully for the party's presidential nomination in 2008 and 2012, Paul had attracted notable media attention over 2012–15 for his positions against National Security Agency bulk data collection of communications, drone strikes and the PATRIOT Act, and for saying that it was a "mistake to topple" Saddam. Such positions and his confrontational style, which included lengthy filibusters on the Senate floor and pungent descriptions of fellow Republican officials, gained him something of a following among libertarians and Tea Party followers. But even Paul adjusted his positions over 2014–15, as the combination of international developments and the exigencies of appealing to the Republican base made anti-interventionism a losing proposition. With the advances made by ISIS, Russian aggression in Ukraine and Chinese cyber-attacks, the Kentucky senator struggled to consolidate his anti-interventionist base while expanding his coalition. After spending 2013–14 as something of a media favorite, including being anointed on the cover of *Time* magazine as the "most interesting man in American politics,"[32] Paul rapidly ceded that status to Trump as he gradually drifted out of the conversation and down the polls through 2015–16.

Paul's decline graphically illustrated the striking, if not surprising, extent to which opposition to Obama's foreign policy was universal. Certainly, important policy distinctions could be drawn among the candidates. But these significant nuances over immigration, surveillance and how best to combat groups like ISIS – though hugely amplified by profound differences of tone, rhetoric and style – appeared like counting angels on the heads of a pin behind the much more substantial anti-Obama common ground. Opposition to the Iran deal was universal (including Paul), Rubio describing it to Secretary of State John Kerry at a Senate Foreign Relations Committee hearing in July 2015 as "terrible." Although some candidates such as Cruz and Rubio pledged reversing the deal from "day one" of their presidency others, such as Bush and Trump, acknowledged that an immediate action was neither feasible nor necessarily prudent. Antipathy toward Putin was manifest (Trump's "bromance" with the Russian leader being the conspicuous exception that proved the rule), as was suspicion of China. Support for Israel was sacrosanct. Most were strong free trade advocates. None offered the type of paleo-conservative, "America First" approach of Pat Buchanan in 1992 and 1996, although Trump expressed a nationalist/populist position in being open to tariffs on China in retaliation for its currency manipulation and devaluations, and Cruz – perhaps unintentionally – once used the provocatively loaded term "America First" to summarize his less reflexively interventionist approach to national security in the GOP debate of December 15 in Las Vegas.

Although Graham (who went on to endorse Bush) was the only candidate openly to endorse US ground troops against ISIS, all pledged a stronger national defense, support for the intelligence community and closer relationships with allies (though typically, Trump was alone in stressing that he would force such allies to adequately compensate the United States for its protection).[33] At the May 2015 South Carolina Freedom Summit, Rubio even answered a question on his ISIS strategy by referring to the Liam Neeson movie *Taken*: "We will look for you, we will find you, and we will kill you" (an approach that Trump extended to encompass the families of targeted terrorists, in breach of the Geneva Conventions). Rubio's *Foreign Affairs* essay, "Restoring American Strength," outlined a combative strategy that few Republicans other than Trump, Paul and, to an extent, Cruz would find much of substance with which to object.[34] While, as one would expect of the candidate initially regarded as the establishment frontrunner and the latest dynastic expression of the Bush family's conviction in "no child left behind," Jeb's views put him squarely in the middle of the GOP consensus on foreign affairs that formed as his brother had reshaped US engagement with the world after 9/11. Bush stumbled to explain for several days in May 2015 whether he would have authorized the Iraq War based on intelligence that emerged after the conflict began. Ultimately, he said he would not have ordered US troops into Iraq. But he remained a strong defender of the "surge," arguing that American forces ultimately restored order to the country. Delivering a speech on combating terrorism at the Reagan Library on August 11, 2015, Bush quoted the GOP icon in noting that, "What we are facing in ISIS and its ideology is, to borrow a phrase, the focus of evil in the modern world."[35] Again, none of his fellow Republicans – not least Trump and Cruz – would disagree.

One way of reading the runes is to employ the typology of Republican foreign policy fissures offered by Colin Dueck,[36] who divides the party into four categories: *realists* favoring the prudent use of force and diplomacy to achieve narrowly defined national interests; *hawks* who believe in the utility of military power and occasional need for armed intervention overseas; *nationalists* concerned with preserving America's sovereignty and avoiding diplomatic concessions to overseas adversaries; and *anti-interventionists* keen to avoid military conflicts abroad. On that basis, the bulk of 2016 candidates fell into rather blurred categories of hawks and nationalists. Although he sought to claim the mantle of Reaganite "realism" as his own throughout 2012–16, only Paul was clearly in the anti-interventionist camp, though Cruz also advocated a less interventionist position than his fellow Cuban-American senator, Rubio. Trump condemned America losing "stoopid" wars in the Middle East but, like Cruz, faced the problem of squaring an unequivocal commitment to defeating ISIS with a rhetorical embrace of a more selective interventionism and a fluid but sometimes narrow definition of the national interest. One could perhaps place Bush, Kasich and Christie tentatively in conservative realist category, less on their public statements and speeches than on the basis that the three of them would be most likely to be pragmatic rather than ideological in office (as would Mitt Romney had he been elected in 2012, despite his self-described "severe conservative" credentials). But none of the candidates had amassed either a governing record or a public reputation that fell clearly into the quintessentially realist mold of figures such as Richard Nixon, Henry Kissinger, George H. W. Bush, James Baker, Brent Scowcroft or Colin Powell (or, indeed, the pre-9/11 George W. Bush and Condoleezza Rice).

Indeed, one of the most noteworthy developments of the Republican Party since the end of the Cold War has been the steady decline in the ranks of realists among its foreign policy intellectuals and associated organizations. The influential and vital tradition still exists, and is well represented in journals such as *The National Interest* and *The American Interest*. Groups like the John Hay Initiative and Americans for Peace, Prosperity and Security also provided intellectual ballast for a conservative internationalism. But, as Dueck argues, the bulk of the GOP is neither Jeffersonian, Hamiltonian, dovish, nor truly anti-interventionist in its foreign policy approach. The party base is essentially Jacksonian. Although the supposedly nativist and anti-interventionist Tea Party excited a lot of attention both in the United States and outside over Obama's presidency, it remains a much misunderstood phenomenon. On foreign policy, especially, the growth of the Tea Party was often treated as an expression of a right-wing anti-interventionism or, on some accounts, isolationism. But to the extent that foreign affairs impinged on the Tea Party's predominantly domestic focus, it was invariably related to the issue of US sovereignty. The rise and fall of Paul attested more to the continued marginality of the anti-interventionist strain in Republicanism than its growing centrality. Even at its brief height in the media after 2012, there were and probably remain no more than twenty–thirty Republican members of Congress in the noninterventionist camp. But the eclipse of Paul by Trump and Cruz posed inherent problems for a party committed to internationalism and a strong defense: is selectively hawkish nationalism – a "tougher" and more assertive foreign policy than Obama, but a less forward-leaning one than George W. Bush, premised on a narrowly parsimonious conception of the American interest – both coherent and feasible?

Moreover, while costly nation-building and international improvement missions are for the time being unpopular to the point of being politically toxic, the Wilsonian element in American foreign policy – including Republican approaches – is arguably too deeply rooted to disappear altogether. No serious, or viable, contender for the presidency is going to revive the "freedom agenda" of George W. Bush or place democracy promotion and "ending tyranny" at the heart of foreign policy. But nor are American values and ideals likely to be indefinitely relegated to the afterthought they became under the Obama administration. Of the candidates from which the Republican nominee, and a possible Republican president, would most conceivably emerge – Trump, Cruz, and Rubio – the first two offered the clearest expression of Jacksonianism, or American nationalism. Trump's foreign policy stance proved, like his approach more generally, less a coherent set of carefully considered policy ideas than a Curate's Egg of populist bombast ("We don't win any more", "When I'm president, we'll win so much!"), protectionist leanings and aggressive nationalism (encompassing a "beautiful" wall on the Mexican border that Mexico would pay for and a moratorium on all Muslims entering the United States). Yet it proved no less potent for that in its tapping of a visceral popular frustration, anti-elitism and anti-intellectualism, especially among the white working class. But – the opaque and not entirely coherent New Yorker aside – the ideological differences among the leading candidates were nonetheless really ones of degree, not nature, notwithstanding the vastly different temperamental and character aspects that would inevitably influence their decision making in office.

History should of course make us cautious about inferring future policies from current dispositions. Politics, including geopolitics, is more art than science. And much as presidents have been surprised and often disappointed by the behavior of the Supreme Court Justices whom they nominate once on the bench, events can habitually see commanders in chief depart from prepared scripts. After all, George W. Bush's second term as president arguably had more in common with Obama's first than his own. It was during the Bush 2005–09 years when the United States began to reach out diplomatically to Iran, pressed the Israelis and Palestinians on peace and refused to bomb Syria's (North Korean-built) nuclear reactor. "Black swans" can occur that puncture apparent equilibriums. Nonetheless, with that qualification in mind, it seems reasonable to assume that if the White House is occupied by a Republican from 2017, a more strategically assertive approach is likely to be adopted, the extent of this being more a matter of degree and coherence, depending on whether the more conservative internationalist/"establishment" (Rubio) or populist/nationalist (Trump/Cruz) nominee prevails. In most instances, the operative question is less whether such a change would occur than how far geopolitics and domestic constraints temper the extent of its application.

The Democratic Party
How, then, do the prospects for renewal fare if "45" is another Democrat? Arguably, less well than with a Republican White House. But not necessarily poorly. Only the most complacent Obama loyalists or the most dyed-in-the-wool partisan opponents of the president can confidently entertain the notion of the administration's policies remaining more or less unchanged under another Democratic presidency. Moreover, a Hillary Clinton White House could, in many respects, be a more reliably internationalist – if not necessarily a more "muscular" presidency - than a Trump or Cruz alternative.

Non-Americans, especially Europeans, frequently favor Democrats in US presidential elections. This is largely because they tend to regard Democrats and

Republicans respectively as the Dr. Jekyll and Mr. Hyde of American internationalism. They hope and imagine that the former will be closer to "Venusian"
positions on international matters than what they regard as reflexively belliger-
ent Republicans, who appear – as Churchill said of John Foster Dulles – like
a bull who carries around with him his own china shop (and whose promises
to make America grate again invariably succeed). Although cynics might suggest that this is a triumph of hope over experience, to the extent that the era
of Cold War liberals such as Truman, JFK and Lyndon B. Johnson is long over,
they are broadly correct. "Militant liberalism" has become a misnomer in a
party whose activists tend to regard macro-aggression abroad as illegitimate
as micro-aggressions on campus. A *New York Times-CBS* poll of delegates to
the two parties' national conventions in 2008, for example, found that 80 percent of Republican delegates and 70 percent of Republican voters agreed that
the United States "did the right thing in taking military action against Iraq."
Only 2 percent of Democratic delegates, and 14 percent of Democratic voters,
agreed.[37] The still-born 2016 presidential candidacy of former US Senator Jim
Webb (D-VA), and the marginalization of Senator Joe Lieberman (D-CT) in the
Democratic Party, from his selection by Al Gore as vice-presidential candidate
in 2000 to his defeat in a party primary in Connecticut in 2006, also illustrated
powerfully the extent to which the party has become increasingly uncomfortable with hawkish internationalism. Driven by demographic and ideological
changes, the Democratic Party base is certainly much more dovish, domesti-
cally focused and progressive than the GOP.

The party's elite officials, Beltway establishment and ambitious elected officials nonetheless tend to be considerably less instinctively anti-war and more
reflexively internationalist than its base. For every Democratic presidential
nominee, this creates a difficult balancing act between appealing to an activist
base and attracting more moderate voters in a general election. The contemporary political reality is therefore rather more complicated than a neat and tidy
partisan divide pitting "cowboy" Republicans against "dovish" Democrats.
Although some scholars denigrate the Republicans as lacking moderates and
resembling "a heavily muscled body without a head,"[38] the Obama foreign
policy has equally caused concern that the Democrats in turn are too easy to
depict as resembling a brain without a spine. Three features should qualify the
latter notion.

First, as Obama's presidency demonstrated, Democrats can prove at least
as difficult to US allies as Republicans, albeit in different ways. Several allies
expressed dismay as to the relative absence of American engagement under
Obama and certainly, it is difficult to think of a US relationship with an ally
that was as close as, for instance, that of Reagan and Thatcher, George H. W.
Bush and Helmut Kohl, Bill Clinton or George W. Bush and Tony Blair.

Second, for all their qualified embrace of "hard power" and greater emphasis on "soft" or "smart" power (the unobjectionable notion that America
should coordinate its military, economic and diplomatic resources when it

acts abroad), Democrats are not averse to the use of coercive diplomacy or military force. Bill Clinton used force more than Reagan, after all, while Al Gore was arguably the most hawkish member of the Clinton administration when it came to issues such as Iraq. Those with short memories who view George W. Bush as the incarnation of American callousness might also recall the vehement anti-Americanism that attended Clinton's bombing of Iraq in 1998, his making regime change official US policy with the signature of the 1998 Iraq Liberation Act and the economic sanctions that were widely charged as responsible for the deaths of thousands of Iraqis during his presidency, his use of rendition, and the "illegal" (i.e. non-UN-sanctioned) war in Kosovo. While the Clinton practice of using the military for humanitarian interventions was largely discarded by Obama – with the partial exception of Libya – a Democratic presidency is likely to be forced by conviction or necessity to utilize US forces in conflict once more.

Third, as issues such as trade, China, Israel and Iran illustrated during Obama's presidency, the Democratic Party is divided over foreign policy. On the one hand, some on the party's left wing believe that Obama's foreign policy was too much like that of his predecessor as president and too tough in relation to international adversaries. In Pew and Gallup opinion surveys on issues such as drone strikes and counterterrorism, military spending, ISIS, Iran and Afghanistan, a large percentage of the Democratic Party feels that Obama has been too hawkish. On the other hand, those party officials concerned with electability are apt to adopt more moderate positions. Perhaps the most notable instance of this occurred when Chuck Schumer, the senator for New York and widely tipped to succeed Harry Reid (D-NV) as the party's leader in the Senate, opposed Obama's Iran deal in August 2015. Issuing a thoughtful explanation, Schumer explained his "Martian" rationale on the basis that:

Iran will not change, and under this agreement it will be able to achieve its dual goals of eliminating sanctions while ultimately retaining its nuclear and non-nuclear power. Better to keep US sanctions in place, strengthen them, enforce secondary sanctions on other nations, and pursue the hard-trodden path of diplomacy once more, difficult as it may be.[69]

How the internal party battle plays out will be intriguing. Despite the multiple scandals that dogged her (and her husband), Hillary Clinton was long held to be the party's presumptive 2016 presidential nominee. Few figures have personified the positioning dilemma on foreign affairs more strongly. In 2008, it was in many respects her relatively hawkish record that hampered her struggle against Obama for the party's presidential nomination. Although she subsequently apologized for her 2002 vote to authorize the Iraq War, it remained an albatross around her neck, and contrasted with Obama's consistent opposition. In 2002, a yes vote had been considered the safe thing for Democrats to do. They had been attacked for years by Republicans for being "weak" on national security and many feared that, especially post-9/11, if the war looked anything like the 1991 Gulf War – brief, successful and relatively bloodless, at least for Americans – then a "no" vote would reinforce those criticisms. Every major Democrat contemplating a future presidential run voted yes, including John Kerry, John Edwards, Joe Biden and Clinton. But that turned out to be politically damaging. The American public turned against the war and Kerry spent much of his unsuccessful 2004 presidential campaign trying to explain why he had voted yes (though it is worth noting that of those who voted on the basis of Iraq in the 2004 general election, over 80 percent supported Kerry). Had Clinton not supported the war, she, rather than Obama, would likely have been the 2008 Democratic nominee and president. The Iraq vote did not determine the nomination but created the opening for someone who had opposed the war.

In some respects, of course, 2002 was very much "history" and Clinton could adopt the philosophy of Marshal Foch toward her party: "My center is giving way, my right is in retreat, situation excellent, I shall attack." Most intra-party divisions focused more on domestic than foreign policy. On the former, Clinton proposed a conventional progressive agenda on immigration reform, gun control, voting rights, college affordability, regulating the financial sector and economic pocketbook concerns, such as expanding paid leave. But while Clinton attempted to tack to the left on the former, there was little evidence of a new or distinctive approach on international affairs. Although she did endorse Obama's Iran deal, equivocated over trade and argued for the lifting of the US trade embargo on Cuba, for the most part her approach was loyalist and tribal. In August 2015, for example, she criticized Republicans for "cowboy diplomacy," "reckless warmongering" and policies where "ideology trumps evidence" while calling for those evergreen philosopher's stones, "progress" and "fresh thinking."

Republicans naturally attempted to tie Clinton to Obama on foreign affairs, frequently referring to the Obama-Clinton or Obama-Clinton-Kerry foreign policy. But this conveniently ignored two factors. One was the extent to which Clinton had been excluded from foreign policy formulation under the hyper-centralized and politicized White House. She served loyally as an eloquent and effective ambassador for Obama's foreign policy, and holds the record for the most countries visited by a secretary of state, 112 (although her total of 956,733 air miles fell short of the 1.06 million logged by Condoleezza Rice).[49] But she was often exempt – as were other principals – from its actual formulation. Second, it was clear from her own memoirs, those of other administration insiders, and press coverage, that Clinton sided with the more interventionist-inclined members of the administration on issues such as Libya, Syria and Russia. Even in October 2015, she bucked the consensus within her own party by advocating a US-enforced "no-fly zone" in northern Syria to protect civilians.

Although the fluidity in her positioning was a constant, most of her political career suggested a fairly hawkish internationalism that was somewhat to the right of Obama and much more in line – on foreign, if not domestic, policy – with the approach of her husband as president. Given her age, pedigree and experience, it is difficult to imagine a Clinton presidency adopting an unconventional or radical approach to foreign policy. Her high unfavorability ratings and continuing problems with the FBI investigation into her private e-mail account notwithstanding, Clinton's electoral dilemma was that her record as secretary of state tied her to the Obama administration, but her own preferences appeared somewhat more hawkish than both the president's and the party's activist base. As Bob Gates revealed in his own memoir, Clinton had admitted to opposing the surge in Iraq in 2007 purely for electoral expediency – regretting her 2002 vote to authorize the Iraq War and looking ahead to the 2008 primaries and caucuses – rather than from strategic calculations. A September 9, 2015, speech at the Brookings Institution in Washington also signaled careful but clear criticism of Obama for his hesitancy on foreign issues. As one analysis aptly summarized the positioning of defining her own standpoint while needing Obama's electoral coalition to win the White House:

Clinton of course is well aware of this feeling, and eager to reassure leftist anti-war activists that she has no fundamental disagreement with them. This helps explain her demonization of Republicans as warmongers, to rally her own base. But it puts her in a difficult position insofar as she must simultaneously lay out a serious case on national security heading into 2016. Whether she can walk this tightrope remains to be seen. Altogether, when it comes to foreign policy, Clinton wants to have it both ways. She wants shared credit for whatever went right internationally under Obama – but no responsibility for all that went wrong. She wants left-liberal party activists to believe her heart is with them – but she also wants genuine moderates to believe the same thing. She wants credit for being hawkish and tough on national security – except when it's more useful to be a dove.[41]

Of Clinton's challengers, foreign policy was not a major issue of division. Jim Webb, the former senator for Virginia, had served as navy secretary under Reagan, and had a position that sought to combine military strength with anti-interventionism – he opposed the Iran deal agreed by President Obama – but dropped out of the race in October 2015, along with Lincoln Chaffee. Bernie Sanders, the self-proclaimed democratic socialist, appeared to be in a similar position – having voted against the Iraq resolution but for authorizing force in Kosovo and after 9/11 – as did Martin O'Malley. Sanders, for example, did not disavow the use of drones for targeted assassinations, though he claimed the cost-benefit calculation in each case needed careful consideration. Although a stay-the-course candidacy by Joe Biden would likely have increased the salience of Obama's failures in the 2016 election, the vice president ruled out a run at the end of October 2015.

Again, if one seeks to classify Democrats, the party's Jeffersonian and Hamiltonian tendencies have eclipsed its Wilsonian and Jacksonian elements. While one can easily point to Democrats who believe in human rights and democracy promotion, few now make that a center piece of their approach.

Even Susan Rice and Samantha Power, for whom combating genocide was a high priority, hardly advanced that agenda in office (the problematic case of Libya aside). Similarly, the Jacksonian element in the party has become steadily diminished in numbers and influence from the era in which Henry "Scoop" Jackson could mount a serious bid for its nomination in 1976. According to the fourfold typology developed by Kurt Campbell and Michael O'Hanlon,[42] the party can be divided into: *hard power advocates*, Scoop Jackson Democrats comfortable with military force and occupied more by hard than soft security issues; *globalists* focused on problems caused by globalization, broader definitions of security and uneasy with using military force; *modest power Democrats* who want America to retrench and refocus at home, viewing Clinton Democrats as "Republican-lite"; and *global rejectionists*, old style leftists, labor unions and environmentalists, prevalent in the blogosphere and academy. On that reading, Clinton hovers between a hard power advocate and globalist while all her challengers bridge the globalist/modest power Democrat categories. None – not even Sanders – fully or properly stands as a global rejectionist/McGovernite. Moreover, influential think tanks of the center-left, such as the Center for a New American Security, have offered analyses that critique Obama policies from a more hawkish perspective.

Or put another way, one can draw a divide between liberal interventionists and left-liberals/radicals. For the former, liberalism and legalism can transcend nationalism with enlightened global institutions and legal bodies, anchored on principles of formal equality. For the latter, the rise of the BRICS and the return of a multipolar world can temper American arrogance and discipline its spasmodic use of military force. A unipolar power can afford not to be constrained by cost-benefit rationality or strategic calculus, a license for threat invention and inflation and all manner of costly violent adventurism. Since a global imbalance of power structurally protects, if not guarantees, the irrationality of US power, correcting the imbalance is just. Some may believe, with Oliver Stone, that a Henry Wallace candidacy would have won the White House in 1948 had he not been deposed as FDR's vice president in 1944 and a similarly left-leaning figure could do so now (Wallace did of course run in the four-horse race of 1948, being soundly rejected and polling some 1.1 million votes out of 48 million cast). But the fact remains that we are not going to see a *Code Pink* or *Move On* dyspeptic Democratic president in the White House, nor a Democratic administration that believes every American conflict must be fought by the Marquis of Queensberry rules. It is one thing for candidates to run for Washington by running against Washington. It is another to run for the position of commander in chief by running against American internationalism. Even Obama, whose personal biography and college views appeared to trend in the direction of global rejectionism, appreciated the electoral dead-end that route offered.

In purely partisan terms, the Democratic Party benefited greatly from the end of the Cold War. This significantly changed the focus of presidential elections away from foreign and national security policy. The 1992, 1996, 2000, 2008 and 2012 presidential elections were not about foreign policy. But even here, successful presidential candidates recognized that, even if only at a subconscious level, American voters are still assessing whether the aspirants fit the profile of a commander in chief. In 1992, Bill Clinton made a concerted effort to criticize George H. W. Bush from a more hawkish stance on issues such as Bosnia, Iraq and China. In 2008 and 2012, Obama benefited from the perceived overreach and incompetence of the Bush administration and enjoyed ratings on foreign affairs close to John McCain, and better than Mitt Romney, respectively. Neither Clinton nor Obama then – nor Al Gore in 2000 – could credibly be portrayed as "soft" on national security.

2016 suggests a similar dynamic. If anything, though, the incentives to demonstrate "strength" when the phone rings in the White House at 3 a.m. – to reprise Clinton's 2008 campaign ad – are probably even greater. First, and most notably, even if the presidential election is not dominated by foreign policy, it is likely to prove a more salient issue for voters than in most recent presidential contests (2004 aside). The reemergence of terrorism as a concern, the aggression of Russia and China, the continuing dilemmas posed by Iran and the Middle East meltdown and the vexing trade-off between guns and butter are all issues that force their way onto campaign agendas. Second, Republicans clearly perceive – rightly or wrongly – that the Obama record on foreign and national security policy is one that creates an opening for them. A Democratic candidate will be pulled in different directions, by the imperative of loyalty to the incumbent president and the need to demonstrate independence in crafting his or her own approach to international affairs. But however much the Obama record may be defended, the agenda will have moved on from 2008 and 2012. It is not going to be about ending unsuccessful wars, nor will it occur against the backdrop of the assassination of the world's most wanted terrorist or the tide of war allegedly receding. Instead, it will be about what to do about threats that are growing. Given the proclivities and preferences of the US public, it is difficult to envisage how a successful presidential candidacy can be mounted on a platform of blanket anti-interventionism. The debate is more likely to hinge on the extent to which a more multilateralist-inclined Democratic mantra – working with allies, through international organizations and mostly eschewing direct use of US forces – trumps a more unilateralist-leaning Republican approach emphasizing a strong defense, coercive diplomacy and the selective use of American force.

Conclusion

Despite the best efforts of the Obama administration to prove otherwise, the US strategic personality has not fundamentally altered since 2009. And despite the rise of Trump within the Republican Party and what E. J. Dionne perhaps prematurely describes as the GOP's "Trumpification,"[43] autopsies of American internationalism remain decidedly premature. Public opinion may not always exhibit the wisdom of Solomon but the robustness of internationalist preferences has stayed intact and transcended events and changes in control of the White House. Even after 9/11, the Great Recession and the Afghan and Iraq Wars, there has been no upsurge in popular sentiment to retreat behind a Fortress America. Most Americans do not want to be the world's policeman but nor do they want the United States to become a follower in international affairs. Nor are Americans squeamish about a tough line on counterterrorism. To a remarkable extent, not least considering the disproportionate costs of its global role and impact of recent wars, opinion remains mostly internationalist, pro-alliances and judicious but not dovish about the use of military force. While not determinative of policy, it sets broad parameters and constraints and acts as a moderating force on both parties who might otherwise pursue more polarized alternatives. For Republicans, public opinion serves as a break on more assertive tendencies; for Democrats, a political levee against periodically threatening tides of disinclination to proactive involvement abroad.

That does not mean, as many outside the United States are apt to imagine, that changes of president amount to no more than "meet the new boss/same as the old boss." Notwithstanding the internationalist inclinations of the public and political class, politics is not going to cease at the water's edge. Imagining that faraway country is chasing a will o' the wisp. There exists substantial division over foreign affairs among the attentive public. Moreover, this is not merely an artifact of the tribalism that is part and parcel of two-party politics or even the recent ideological "sorting" of liberals and conservatives into the Democratic and Republican parties. For all of the problems that attend opinion surveys and answers partly reflecting the way that questions are phrased, there now exists compelling evidence of a significant partisan difference on issues from Israel to international trade and foreign aid. This finds ample expression on Capitol Hill. Where presidents actively require congressional support, partisan politics can hamper the pursuit of the national interest, especially in conditions of divided party control of the White House and Congress. "Sometimes party loyalty asks too much," JFK once remarked. It is not a sentiment often heard today.

But the severity of this should not be overstated. The Cold War was neither a succession of victories nor a tranquil era of bipartisan comity. Moreover, a determined president, able and willing to dedicate political capital to foreign policy priorities, can typically prevail. That was the case with the surge in 2007–08, Obama's gaining trade promotion authority in 2015 over the objections of most congressional Democrats and the approval of the Iran deal over the objections of most Republicans. The Netanyahu speech and Cotton letter backfired, alienating Democrats who might otherwise have been more open to opposing even their own president. Instead, the reorientation of US foreign policy toward Iran was approved by the minority in Congress without a substantive vote. Clearly, the difficulty in marshalling supermajorities to overcome filibusters and presidential vetoes is a powerful impediment to law-makers making effective the legislative authority that remains entirely theirs under the Constitution. Although there is much to criticism of congressional micromanagement, presidential unilateralism has a particular force on foreign affairs. That is unlikely to change.

The remarkable 2016 race in many respects overturned the conventional wisdom that "the party decides" and that Democrats want to fall in love with their nominee while Republicans want to fall in line. With the insurgent, anti-establishment and populist strain unusually intense, that wisdom was partially reversed as the nomination struggles appeared part-mutiny as much a campaign, especially in the convulsive Republican Party. But while there is a strong case that Obama has changed his party more than his country, the Obama Doctrine appeared well past its "best-before" date. And while this does not imply an imminent revival of the Bush Doctrine – under yet another Bush or otherwise – the prospects for moving beyond retrenchment and accommodation, especially with a Republican president, and even with one keen to resurrect the art of the deal, seem strong. Even with a Democrat in the Oval Office, and especially with Hillary Clinton, geopolitical imperatives are likely to compel intervention-ist measures in the national interest that may run powerfully against the dovish grain of the party's base.

After Obama, we can therefore reasonably expect that the "pendulum" of US global involvement will once again tilt away from an insular, parochial and reactive focus in the opposite direction. That does not mean that American leaders will again proclaim it their mission to defend freedom worldwide, as Truman and Kennedy did during the Cold War and Bush did for a time after 9/11. It does imply that there is reason not only to hope for, but also anticipate, a more proactive, forward-leaning and strategic change in direction post-Obama. But that also relies on the forty-fifth president employing the full array of hard and soft power resources rather than tailoring foreign policies for a "post-American" world. And that, in turn, means refuting, rather than accepting, the premise of US decline.

4

Reversing declinism: toward a second American century?

3 6 NOTES
P. 135

If neither public opinion nor partisan polarization preclude a revival of US strategy after Obama, might global realities nonetheless make that prospect mere wishful thinking? Even for many commentators who would prefer otherwise, the brutal truth is that America is in a steady but inexorable decline. Obama may publicly have denied this for political reasons but his actual policies were founded upon the premise. On this view, Obama was merely the first American president to embrace having to deal with the process of managing national decline, much as successive British prime ministers after World War II were resigned to administering the end of empire. Integral to this was a lighter US footprint abroad, a delegation of authority to other surrogate states and organizations to lead, and a scaling back of international commitments. To his supporters, Obama made a sound fist of retrenching gradually and accustoming both Americans and the wider world to a more circumspect, reticent US role. Neither genocide in Syria, terrorist attacks in the United States nor the dismemberment of a sovereign state in Europe could disturb the equanimity of a White House committed to achieving a new global equilibrium.

Ambitious politicians on the presidential campaign trail may protest otherwise and US policymakers may feel uncomfortable adjusting to the new normal of a loss of power and prestige. But, for declinists, the global balance is shifting rapidly and America can no longer, as Cassius put it in *Julius Caesar*, "bestride the narrow world like a Colossus." True, the United States still possesses the largest national economy, a huge share of international trade, a vast investment of overseas capital and the most powerful military. But these assets no longer translate into the patterns of global influence that America once enjoyed. Optimists might view Washington's glass as more half full than half empty. But the halcyon days when China needed the United States to balance against Russia, when Moscow impassively watched NATO expand to its borders or when Iranian ambitions were intimidated by an American aircraft carrier presence in the Persian Gulf are long gone (the United States, for the first time in several years, had no carrier group there at all for two months in the fall of 2015). The inevitable rise of other great powers, the historical reckoning of Sunni-Shia tensions in the Middle East, and the hollowing out of the state through globalization have rebalanced the international system in ways that no single nation could forestall or reverse. That rebalancing in turn has systematically eroded the ability of the United States to dominate geopolitics, geoeconomics or geostrategy. That does not mean that the rocks of multipolarity are beckoning America's Titanic. It does imply that Washington can neither maintain its own "exceptional" role nor consistently exercise traditional modes of global leadership. Campaign rhetoric may reliably promise messages of national restoration as a sound political and psychological tactic ("Make America Great Again!"). But though the United States remains top dog and retains primacy, it is, as it were, not your father's (or even your grandfather's) primacy.

By the latter stages of the Obama administration, some of its senior members were giving vivid expression – intentionally or otherwise – to this sentiment. Seeking to build congressional support for the nuclear agreement with Tehran, Secretary of State John Kerry declared that American allies would "look at us and laugh" if the United States were to abandon the deal and subsequently ask its partners to back a more aggressive posture against Iran. Not only would US global credibility be undermined but the dollar's position as the world's reserve currency would also be threatened. "It's not going to happen overnight. But I'm telling you, there's a huge antipathy out there," Kerry warned, toward US leadership. Highlighting efforts by Russia and China to join forces with rising, nonaligned powers, he observed that, "there's a big bloc out there, folks, that isn't just sitting around waiting for the United States to tell them what to do.[2] Combined with immense economic and social strains at home, the nascent counterbalancing pressuring America appeared to render its primacy more superficial than substantive, framed by a dull but persistent throb of national anxiety. Perhaps, like the Vikings and Mayans previously, Americans have been complacently authoring their own downfall by destroying the environment on which their power depended, in the US case through overstretch abroad and indebtedness at home? Or, much as – according to the Talmud – the Romans were able to conquer Jerusalem and drive the Jews into exile because of the debilitating divisions among them, have America's internal rifts allowed others to take advantage of its discord and disunity to eclipse its standing?

If American decline is simply a fact to which the United States had best become accultured and that, if it is occurring, cannot be arrested, crafting post-Obama grand strategy clearly needs to accommodate that new reality. Rather than raging against the dying of the superpower light, the United States can go gently into the good multipolar night. The Obama Doctrine may have even provided the template for a new consensus behind that path. But even if the tectonic plates of international order are shifting in a more plural direction,

America's slow motion self-implosion is far from self-evidently the case. Indeed, notwithstanding that declinism has a long and undistinguished history in relation to the United States, there is an unmistakable *Schadenfreude* to many such accounts. Non-American writers have long predicted the decline and fall of the West in general and the United States in particular, as much in hope as expectation (and from the very founding of the republic). For some Americans too, whose domestic priorities mostly point in a progressive direction (though there are echoes on the paleo-conservative and neo-isolationist right), the decline prognosis provides a conveniently elaborate and compelling rationale for refocusing American energies away from an active global imprint. Cynics might suggest there was more than a smidgeon of this implicit in the Obama pivot to America. Whereas, for some of the right, soaring deficits have been a means of "starving the beast" (precluding new domestic social programs), for some on the left the logic of deficits is instead to starve the appetite to go abroad to seek monsters to destroy (cutting defense). "Offshore balancing," in realist parlance – keeping US forces over the horizon – is the logical strategic destination of Obama's new navigation of the ship of state.

Whatever the merit in that cynicism, there seem three good reasons to question the validity of the declinist argument, which this chapter elaborates in turn.

First, while it is obvious that the United States faces very serious difficulties at home and that public opinion about America's identity and future is far from optimistic, there is also cause for confidence in Americans' ability to overcome their problems. Conventional wisdom typically blames the gridlocked political system or a "corrupt" political class for many of the current maladies and the seeming inability to find solutions to remedy them. But the more prosaic truth is that Americans are divided over innumerable issues – closely and sometimes deeply, in other cases less dramatically so – and the shape of American politics is working these divisions out, slowly, haphazardly and incrementally, much as the founding fathers intended. That does not make the divisions any less real or intense. America faces profound domestic problems (although whether and how these compare to the fractures over civil rights, crime and war that threatened to tear America apart during the 1960s and 1970s is highly questionable). But the best way to approach issues surrounding American decline is not to judge too hastily or emphatically from temporary trends and instead locate them in their appropriate historical and comparative contexts.

Second, although it is true that the "rise of the rest" is occurring, the speed and extent to which this is displacing the United States is open to challenge. In one obvious but important sense, America is not losing "control" of global order because it never possessed such control in the first place. At the apex of its post-World War II economic dominance and enormous expenditure of GDP on defense, the United States was unable to defeat North Korea or defend South Vietnam, pacify the Middle East or even overthrow the communist regime in Cuba. Periodic panics over America's eclipse by the Soviet Union, the European Economic Community and Japan punctuated its postwar ascendancy. The partial erosion of America's relative economic standing owed much to the recovery of Western Europe (especially [West] Germany) and Japan that the Marshall Plan deliberately facilitated. Moreover, while some analysts suggest a linear rise of the BRICS (Brazil, Russia, India, China and South Africa) and others, these are far from foreordained. On multiple dimensions, the political, economic and social problems that America's rivals and adversaries face are at least as great as – and some persuasively argue, far more severe than – those confronting the United States. In short, as a nation-state looking to the future, whose problems would you rather have? Framed in this fashion, the relative strengths of the United States, and the more acute problems confronting other powers – allies, adversaries and "frenemies" in between – appear more enduring and consequential. America may have lost some of its sizzle but still has the steak.

Third, if the preceding arguments are sound, this leaves us with the question of agency. If the economic determinism and historical materialism that underscore most declinist accounts are correct, then there is little point in policymakers doing anything but passively adjusting to new global realities. But the history of economic determinism is pervaded by examples of explanatory and predictive error, where peoples did not behave as they were supposed to. America cannot make its path in the world today through splendid isolation any more than previously and, as the last chapter documented, most Americans are well aware of this and reject either retreating from the world or seeking to dominate it. But the kinds of impediment to US leadership that have been identified by critics of the Obama administration are ones that can be corrected. They are not predominantly structural or systemic in nature but discrete and contingent. The decisions that Americans make at home about putting their house in order and, abroad, in terms of influencing others' choices through foreign and national security policy, will substantially shape the future. That is precisely why the choices offered by the parties in the 2016 presidential and, to a lesser extent, congressional elections matter. Leadership is itself a variable in the world order and global power equation. One need not necessarily agree with Charles Krauthammer's typically provocative argument about the Obama administration, that "decline is a choice," to argue against taking unwise measures that amount to the preemptive geopolitical suicide of the one remaining superpower. Washington can certainly choose to quit its onerous leadership burdens and become a parochial power. But if the United States addresses its key shortcomings, the possibility of remaining *primus inter pares* (first among equals) is the minimum to which it can aspire. The world is, as one American analysis concluded, "still ours to lead."[3]

The case for decline I: America against itself

Whether or not America is in decline is a question about which Americans themselves clearly disagree. As recently as 2011, 54 percent of those polled said the country was in a state of decline, against 42 percent who said it wasn't; a 12 percentage point gap. But by January 2015, a *Wall Street Journal/NBC News* poll found a significant shift, with fewer than half of Americans saying the country was declining: 49 percent said it was, against 48 percent who said it was not. Moreover, according to Gallup, although four-fifths of Americans (80 percent) thought the United States was now only one of several leading economic powers, rather than Number One in the world economically, 2015 was the first occasion in over twenty-two years that, by the narrowest majority (50–49 percent), more Americans felt it was important for the United States to be Number One than thought it was "not that important." (5)

Famously, the American historian, Richard Hofstadter, claimed that, "It has been our fate as a nation, not to have ideologies but to be one." For those accepting that notion, America was founded on political ideals enshrined in the Declaration of Independence and the US Constitution that make the nation a particularistic community of universal significance and Americans an "exceptional" people. Despite the substantial demographic changes that have transformed America since 1965, and the fissures that find strong expression in the polarized politics of the nation today, there still exists wide agreement that the United States has a unique character because of its history and Constitution that sets it apart from other nations as the greatest in the world. In 2010, this view was shared by 80 percent of Americans, including 73 percent of Democrats, 77 percent of Independents and 91 percent of Republicans. (6) In foreign policy terms, one of the extensions of the belief in American exceptionalism is the notion that, because of its unique status, the United States also has an obligation to be the leading nation in world affairs. Again, despite its internal demographic and social changes, most Americans endorsed this position, 66 percent saying the United States has "a special responsibility to be the leading nation in world affairs." Once more, that belief crossed partisan identifications, encompassing Republicans (73 percent), Democrats (61 percent) and Independents (64 percent), with fairly modest differences. (7)

But at the same time that Americans continued to believe the United States is exceptional, they were also inclined to regard that status as far from secure. Three-quarters of those who believed it is exceptional (62 percent of all Americans) also believed that the country is at risk of losing its unique character. (8) Americans who identify as Republicans were also especially dubious that President Obama regards the United States as exceptional, likely reflecting the opinions of conservative commentators and Republicans such as Mitt Romney and Bobby Jindal who publicly expressed that charge. Only 34 percent of Republicans believed the president thinks that the United States is the greatest country in the world (compared to 83 percent of Democrats and 57 percent of Independents), while over three-fifths (61 percent) believed that he does not. (9) Most US citizens of all political affiliations nonetheless continue to say they are proud to be an American, including 57 percent who professed to being "extremely proud" and 28 percent who were "very proud" (in 2013).

This high level of national pride in being American – substantially greater than other nationalities – has varied only moderately over the previous twelve years since the question was first asked (but has been lower since 2005 than it was in the years prior).Nonetheless, according to Gallup, again in 2013, only 27 percent of Americans believed that the signers of the Declaration of Independence would be pleased by the way the United States had turned out; 71 percent thought that they would be disappointed by today's America

These results confirm that America is in something of a national funk. Immense pride coexists with widespread angst and anger about the nation's future, division over the patriotism of its president and doubt about the fidelity of the contemporary United States to its founders' aspirations. The "land of opportunity" appears to be bound by increasingly rigid social hierarchies and less conducive to social and intergenerational mobility, with individual outcomes largely determined by origins rather than ambition. Social mobility is twice as great for Canada as for the United States while an American child born in the bottom quintile of incomes has only a 4 percent chance of rising to the top quintile.Labor participation is historically low. The median pretax household income in 2011 was $49,103 which, adjusted for inflation, was $4,000 less than that of 2000. Figures from the OECD and World Health Organization documented worrying concerns that the United States in 2010 saw fifteen-year-old Americans rank seventeenth in the world in science and twenty-fifth in mathematics; the United States rated twelfth among developed nations in college education; seventy-ninth in elementary school enrolment; infrastructure was twenty-third in the world; twenty-seventh in life expectancy: eighteenth in diabetes; and first only in comparative obesity levels, number of guns in circulation, largest prison population and accumulated national debt. The Legatum Institute's "Prosperity Index" (a rating combining material wealth and quality of life) of 110 nations documented a decline for the United States from first in 2007 to tenth by 2012. Census Bureau reports also confirmed that more American children lived in poverty in 2015 (22 percent) than at the start of the financial crisis in 2008 (18 percent) and that the share of households reliant on food stamps had more than doubled since 2000. From 2000 to 2013, the share of households receiving aid through the Supplemental Nutrition Assistance Program grew from 6.2 percent to 13.5 percent; from one in sixteen to one in eight Americans.The basic assumption of post-World War II American culture, of rising real incomes and social mobility, no longer applies.

Serious problems also plague the basic national infrastructure of the contemporary United States. Although, for example, America possesses one of the most advanced transportation networks in the world, the system is gradually atrophying. US highways and waterways are hampered by numerous problems, not least congestion, making the transportation of goods in the largest consumer market in the world less than efficient. Decades of neglect have left key infrastructure crumbling and in disrepair. Aging highways, ports and airports are deteriorating while the demands on them are increasing. Bridges throughout the country are vulnerable. Without heavy new investment in transportation networks to keep them competitive, transportation lines may fail while rising costs inhibit economic growth. The knock-on effects in terms of blunting the competitive advantage that the US infrastructure once afforded are potentially severe.

The foundations of America's economy are equally in need of urgent repair. According to the Congressional Budget Office (CBO), if current laws remain unchanged, federal debt held by the public will exceed 100 percent of GDP by 2040 and continue on an upward trajectory relative to the size of the economy that cannot be sustained indefinitely.[14] Add in some $100 trillion of unfunded liabilities of Medicare and Social Security, the growing deficits of the states and the increasing liabilities of public employees' pension schemes, and the sustainability of the national economy is in doubt. The unhappy economic picture is made still gloomier by the $19 trillion national debt, a 20 percent underemployment rate and approximately one in six Americans living below the official poverty level.

Entitlement spending consumes a rapidly growing share of the federal budget. Forty years ago, Medicare and Medicaid accounted for 6 percent of federal spending. In 2014, they accounted for 24 percent. Social Security accounted for another 24 percent of government outlays. The cost of these three major entitlements is expected to grow to 53 percent of the budget in just ten years' time. Entitlement spending will grow because senior citizens comprise a growing share of the population. In addition, despite the passage of the Affordable Care Act (2010), healthcare costs tend to grow faster than the rate of inflation. Thus, most of the cost growth will be in Medicare and Medicaid, although Social Security will also consume its greatest share ever of the federal budget. By 2043, federal spending on entitlements and net interest payments will exceed federal revenues, meaning funds for any discretionary programs will need be borrowed. And while currently interest rates are extremely low, as they recover, the cost of servicing the national debt will rise dramatically. In 2015, the US government paid $227 billion of interest, or 6.2 percent of the budget. In 2020, the CBO projects that the government will have to pay $548 billion, or 11.5 percent of the budget. By 2025, those numbers will be $827 billion and 13.5 percent, significantly more than the entire defense budget. Together, interest payments and major entitlement spending will consume just under two-thirds of the budget. If Congress and the president do not act, entitlement spending and interest payments will make it impossible to support the armed forces – or any other national priority – without incurring debts that will permanently destabilize the entire US economy.

Politically, the manifestations of American *ennui* are everywhere. In 2012, Pew reported that the "values gap" between Democrats and Republicans was greater than all other attitudinal divides, including those based on race, gender, age or class. Since the Bill Clinton era – hardly short of polarized conflict – and despite the widely acknowledged complexity of contemporary problems,

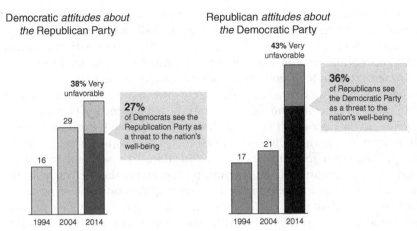

FIGURE 4.1. *Beyond dislike: viewing the other party as a "threat to the nation's well-being."*

Notes: Questions about whether the Republican and Democratic Parties are a threat to the nation's well-being were asked only in 2014.

Republican includes Republican-leaning Independents: Democratic includes Democratic-leaning Independents.

Source: "Political Polarization in the American Public," Pew Research Center, Washington, DC (June, 2014). www.people-press.org/2014/06/12/political-polarization-in-the-american-public/

the proportion of Americans describing themselves as consistently liberal or conservative has doubled. Many progressives and conservatives increasingly self-segregate their entire lives, not just in terms of housing decisions but cultural consumption, lifestyles and even choices of partners and friends. Identity and ideology have coalesced to such an extent that, as Figure 4.1 illustrates, increasing numbers of partisans have come to view the other party as nothing less than a threat to national well-being. Some observers attribute this phenomenon to "asymmetric polarization" and the Republicans shifting strongly to the right of center, as "an insurgent outlier – ideologically extreme; contemptuous of the inherited social and economic policy regime; scornful of compromise; unpersuaded by conventional understanding of facts, evidence, and science; and dismissive of the legitimacy of its political opposition."[15] But others, such as James Pierson, note that forty years ago "moderate" Republicans such as Richard Nixon and Gerald Ford hardly enjoyed convivial relations with Democrats and that, if the GOP has become a coherently "antigovernment" party, it is in part a response to the Democrats becoming a strongly "progovernment" one.[16] At times, and especially during the toxic 2016 presidential campaign, it seems that aspirant presidents loathe half the nation they hope to lead, leaning toward the conclusion of Bertolt Brecht's *The Solution*: "Would it not be easier ... To dissolve the people/And elect another?"

But the partisan frustration fused with a broader and more visceral antipathy toward "Washington" and Wall Street as well. Substantial groups of voters across both left and right are increasingly frustrated with traditional politics and politicians and feel failed by the American system. More than seven in ten say people in politics cannot be trusted, while more than six in ten see the political system as dysfunctional (with sizeable majorities among Republicans, Democrats and Independents in agreement).[17] The 2015–16 insurgent and outsider candidacies of Donald Trump, Ted Cruz, Ben Carson, Carly Fiorina and Bernie Sanders were all fueled by people's anger with the status quo and desire for authenticity in political leaders. Across the ideological spectrum, candidates gained traction by separating themselves from the political and economic system that many everyday Americans view as rigged against them. Much of this anger crossed party lines and was directed at what people see as a concentration of wealth and power that leaves them holding the short end of the stick. Some of the fear and frustration was projected onto particular groups – Mexicans, Muslims and minorities. Apprehension about their economic well-being and the rise of both internal and external challenges to the United States together made them uncomfortable with the country's direction.

To some, the apparent malaise reflected and reinforced nothing less than a broken political culture. Descriptions of this vary. Some point to a "dollarocracy" or "demosclerosis": government that is resistant to change because it is so solicitous toward many minor and discrete, but active and attentive, interests. From corporate firms gaining tax breaks to sugar farmers securing federal price supports, clients thrive in obscurity because of the law of dispersed costs and concentrated benefits, penalizing unaware taxpayers while rewarding well-organized factions. American politics evinces, as Pierson argues, a "shattered consensus" and a new normal. The formerly consensual postwar political order has over time produced a "sorting-out" of Americans into conflicting and hostile political, social and geographical groups. Causing this breakdown are two forces yielding opposing political tribes: first, the mounting inefficiency and cost of government fuels conservative demands for radical shrinkage of the state; and second, the decreasing productivity, growing inequality and perceived unfairness of the economic system animates liberal calls for radical expansion of the state. Long past is the optimistic Keynesian consensus in managed capitalism, which supported the centrist two-party politics of the era from Truman to Nixon and Ford. Intermittent indications of economic recovery and comparative success, such as the leading growth rate of OECD countries and a low 5.1 percent unemployment rate in 2015, cannot suffice to revive public confidence and trust in either business or government (though most Americans still regard "big government" as a greater threat than "big business").

America is therefore headed for either the buffers or a reckoning. The recent years of intense political polarization and conflict are symptoms of economic stagnation and inequality levels not seen since the Gilded Age, the unsustainable growth of government and the crumbling of postwar structures and accommodations that once underpinned US prosperity and power. The cumulative challenges of slow and uneven economic growth, massive public debt and borrowing and the retirement of the "baby boom" generation cannot long be deferred. But the widening gulf between the two political parties and the entrenched power of interest groups and lobbies is making it difficult, if not impossible, to reach agreement on the profound changes in the role of government needed to renew the system and rebalance the economy. Stalemate and inertia prevail in the absence of either coalition making decisive gains or a crisis that transforms the terms of political debate.

Like Piereson, Francis Fukuyama has also argued that in America's contemporary "veto-cracy" only a national crisis can shock a "decaying" nation into properly addressing its deficiencies:

The US political system has decayed over time because its traditional system of checks and balances has deepened and become increasingly rigid. In an environment of sharp political polarization, this decentralized system is less and less able to represent majority interests and gives excessive representation to the views of interest groups and activist organizations that collectively do not add up to a sovereign American people ... The depressing bottom line is that given how self-reinforcing the country's political malaise is, and how unlikely the prospects for constructive incremental reform are, the decay of American politics will probably continue until some external shock comes along to catalyze a true reform coalition and galvanize it into action.[18]

Whether or not that is hyperbolic is unclear. Criticism of American governing arrangements is hardly new. Reflecting widespread dismay at the seeming impossibility of governing in America, President Carter's senior legal counsel, Lloyd Cutler, wrote in 1980 that by fractioning power, preventing accountability and guaranteeing a "permanent centrism":

it is not now possible "to Form a Government." The separation of powers between the executive and legislative branches, whatever its merits in 1793, has become a structure that almost guarantees stalemate today ... the system has succeeded only on the rare occasions when there is an unusual event that brings us together, and creates substantial consensus throughout the country on the need for a whole new program.[19]

That appeared, in retrospect, decidedly premature and the artifact of a particular presidency. Nor is a "permanent centrism" any longer what ails American politics (many critics these days imply, would that it were). Rather, underlying American political conflicts since at least the end of the Cold War, there exists a fundamental clash between what one might term "philosophical conservatism" and "operational liberalism." In terms of the former, antistatism – dislike of "Big Government" and "Washington" – remains the predominant political culture in the United States. But this coexists with a willingness happily to accept government regulation, services and benefits from Social Security to defense contracts. This battle of public philosophies may ultimately be decided one way or another by those "conflicted conservatives" whose belief in small government belies their willingness to support social spending, or by those progressives whose belief in collectivism, in an era of individualism, is ultimately trumped by a lack of money to finance a welfare state on a European model. But at some point, the contending merits of a "red state" and "blue state" model will weigh in one direction or another.

The contemporary European experience certainly has two instructive implications for the United States. First, although welfare states are intuitively preferable to warfare states, the costs of substantial social provision by government hardly yield a postmodern paradise. Social safety nets, guaranteed labor rights and more represent worthy causes but produce unintended consequences. If hiring is made too expensive, there will be less hiring. With the national budget already running large deficits, loading the costs of social policies onto business can be politically appealing. In the United States, the Affordable Care Act, for example, requires firms to provide health insurance for workers; minimum wage increases raise labor costs sharply for many firms; and proposals mandating paid maternity and sick leave achieve similar results. But if labor is priced too high, and workers paid more than they produce, businesses will decline sponsoring their own bankruptcy and will slow or cease hiring.

Second, public policies in liberal democracies are subject to path dependency. Once political and economic commitments are made, with attendant constituencies to defend their vested interests in perpetuating them, they are very hard politically to withdraw, even if they have adverse long-term economic and social side effects. The parlous finances of the blue state model in states like California and municipalities like Detroit amply attests to these difficulties.

It is perhaps tempting in the above light to anticipate that at some stage the need for orderly finances implies that red state solutions may prevail. As noted in the last chapter, the Republican Party is stronger than it has been for many decades, especially at state level. The 54 seats the Republicans won in the Senate in 2014 and the 247 seats in the House represented their highest since the 1928 election, when Herbert Hoover trounced Al Smith; at the local level, the GOP had 31 governors and controlled 68 of 98 partisan state legislatures in 2015–16, its best showing since 1920. The same demographic shifts that have weakened its presidential chances have strengthened it in the states, where most lawmaking in America takes place. In theory, there is popular appeal to the types of economic stances commonly espoused by GOP candidates: simplifying the tax code and reducing taxes, lifting onerous regulations, reforming entitlements and framing a proenergy and progrowth approach to expand the economy. Picket fences appeal more than picket lines. In practice, whether the Republicans can make private enterprise – of which they remain an inconstant friend – work better for the entire nation, and consumers and the struggling middle class especially, remains to be seen.

But the point of resolution of contending partisan visions remains some way distant. It is possible that America is entering a prelude to paralysis in which neither party is strong enough to force through comprehensive reforms.

But ultimately, the question is not whether the United States tackles its internal strains but when. The passage of the two-year budget deal at the end of October 2015 – approved 64–35 in the Senate and 266–167 in the House – was a rare moment of bipartisan compromise offering modest cause for optimism that this might perhaps be sooner rather than later.

The case for decline II: peak America?

If the post-World War II *Pax Americana* ultimately rested on dominating global trade and capital flows, exerting political and economic influence, maintaining global military dominance and spawning an increasingly homogenized global culture, can we truly regard American power as a declining force today? If the eagle is as weary as the Obama experience suggests, is this a temporary phenomenon or a matter of having had its wings permanently clipped?

The oscillations in academic fashion on this question are nothing less than impressive. In 1987, one of the most influential declinist scholars, Paul Kennedy, famously predicted the "imperial overstretch" of the United States in *The Rise and Fall of The Great Powers*.[20] Analyzing the relationship of wealth and power, Kennedy claimed that the United States had fallen into the historical trap that if a state overextends itself strategically, it risks the potential benefits from external expansion being outweighed by the great expense of it all. Yet by 2001, Kennedy was more or less celebrating American power in lyrical terms:

Nothing has ever existed like this disparity of power; nothing ... The *Pax Britannica* was run on the cheap, Britain's army was smaller than European armies, and even the Royal Navy was equal only to the next two navies – right now all the other navies in the world combined could not dent American maritime supremacy. Charlemagne's empire was merely western European in its reach. The Roman Empire stretched farther afield, but there was another great empire in Persia and a larger one in China. There is, therefore, no comparison.[21]

Although Kennedy was to recant this interpretation once again after the Iraq War, and other scholars similarly wrote scathingly of the deeply premature heralding of a unipolar era by American triumphalists, as late as 2008 sober historians were still arguing that US power "on almost any criterion ... now transcends the limits of empire that we have observed in force since the early fifteenth century."[22]

Some might be tempted to infer from the ebb and flow of this debate that the issue is something of an intellectual *cul-de-sac* but, as Table 4.1 demonstrates, the argument over American decline comprises a range of competing interpretations. On the declinist side, the core focus varies between the economic dimensions of American weakness, the systemic problems of unipolarity and inevitable balancing or band-wagoning by other great powers, the over-expansion of America's global footprint (or the costs of "imperialism") and

TABLE 4.1. *Declinists and antideclinists*

Economic declinists	*Economic revivalists*
(Paul Kennedy, Jim O'Neill)	(Carla Norloff, Michael Mandelbaum)
Structural realists	*Structural positionists*
(Christopher Layne, Stephen Walt,	(Josef Joffe, William Wohlforth,
John Mearsheimer, Kenneth Waltz)	Stephen Brooks)
Overexpansionists	*Soft power advocates*
(Noam Chomsky, Andrew Bacevich)	(Joseph Nye, Robert Lieber)
Country/regional enthusiasts	*Benign hegemonists*
(Charles Kupchan, Mark Leonard)	(Robert Kagan, Charles Krauthammer)

Source: Adapted by the author from Eric S. Edelman, "Understanding America's Contested Primacy" Washington, DC: Center for Strategic and Budgetary Assessments (2010).

the allegedly more rational contemporary models of other countries or regions (most commonly China, though for a time the European Union enjoyed its advocates). Antideclinists tend, in almost symmetrical fashion, to run the gamut of similar themes but drawing different conclusions. Thus, rather than focusing on America's economic flaws, revivalists tend to emphasize its comparative strengths and resilience. Structural positionists tend to downplay the scope of other powers counterbalancing the United States while stressing the resilient dimensions and singular properties of American power. In contrast to those claiming overstretch, soft power advocates note the immense and unparalleled appeal of the United States globally, that reliably transcends particular presidencies and foreign policies. Finally, benign hegemonists point to the historically unique nature of American primacy as key to the maintenance of its numerous alliances and enduring global dominance. Sifting through the entrails of this multifaceted debate is difficult but, arguably, there are three dimensions to the declinist case that unite the various stripes from left to right.

First, there is a range of empirical data and examples that attest to the relative decline of the United States compared to other powers in terms of economic clout. Most obviously, the fall in the share of global GDP commanded by the United States and the growth of competitors indicates an overall weakening of the American position. The failures of the US military interventions in Afghanistan and Iraq, despite the expenditure of substantial blood and treasure, confirmed Washington's sharply constrained capacity to command and control other, substantially weaker, nations. Moreover, they suggest the devaluing of America's comparative military advantage in an age of asymmetric war and "unwinnable conflicts."[23] In economic terms, the days when the "Washington consensus" held sway have long passed into the history books, even before the Great Recession raised profound doubts about the "Anglo-Saxon" model of free market capitalism. China's displacement of the United States as the leading trading partner of South America, along with Beijing's growing investments in Africa, suggested the eclipse of US influence even in its own hemisphere.

Second, the shift of global economic power from the West to the East, and Asia in particular, has been accompanied by a devolution of power away from the state itself. The hollowing out of state power renders the very concept of dominance, much less control, deeply problematic for any great power. Technology and communications fragment nations and alliances, making the projection of power more challenging. In turn, this means that the very concept of world order is more elusive than ever since the anarchic and centrifugal elements of global interaction – while not necessarily producing chaos – are powerfully resistant to ordering by any single state or even a group of states.

To some observers, the most dangerous course for America to chart is to respond to these ineluctable trends with alarmism and belligerence rather than strategic patience. Ironically, the experience of the George W. Bush era demonstrated the dangers inherent in trying to "restore" a lost primacy. Far from maintaining Washington's leading role, US policies accelerated the rebalancing of the system. Invading Iraq as (at least in part) an assertion of regional and global primacy, thereby disrupting the regional balance in the Middle East, contributed significantly to the subsequent religious and ethnic strife that weakened the existing state systems, deepened and broadened anti-American attitudes and emboldened Iran. Even prior to Bush, proclaiming victory in the Cold War and extending the US/NATO collective security compact to include Central and Eastern Europe directly contributed to the desire in Moscow to reassert Russian greatness. Demanding a reassertion of American "leadership" has helped to foster the very disintegration of the old system that the same politicians now decry. A strategic tragedy could easily ensue from actions that seem to be driven by "good intentions" but are based on a wishful ignorance of global realities and produce the opposite results.[24]

A more balanced approach would accept that the implications of American decline are not inevitably negative, inasmuch as a careful husbanding of US resources and restrained statecraft can harness sufficient support still to succeed on the world stage. As Fareed Zakaria argued, the uneven "rise of the rest" rather than any domestic American collapse has been responsible for the relative decline of US power across the economic, diplomatic, geopolitical and cultural realms. But while this necessarily entails the emergence of a *post*-American world, this world need not be *anti*-American. For Washington, it is still possible to maintain "leadership" through a more supple and subtle diplomacy that takes account of the changed global environment:

Functions that were once controlled by governments are now shared with international bodies like the World Trade Organization and the European Union. Non-governmental groups are mushrooming every day on every issue in every country. Corporations and capital are moving from place to place, finding the best location in which to do business, rewarding some governments while punishing others. Terrorists like al Qaeda, drug cartels, insurgents, and militias of all kinds are finding space to operate within the nooks and crannies of the international system. Power is shifting away from nation-states, up, down, and sideways. In such an atmosphere, the traditional applications of national power, both economic and military, have become less effective.[25]

Third, if Washington faces any serious nation-state challenge in this new post-American era, it is unquestionably China. In the Chinese case, America faces a rival unlike any other. As Graham Allison observes, "Never before in history has a nation risen so far, so fast, on so many dimensions of power" and in most instances over the past 500 years such rapid and massive change in the balance of power lead to war.[26] China's steep and rapid rise has transformed the global economy. China's economy is now the world's largest or second largest, depending on the analyst and method of measurement, at least two-and-a-half times the size of the next largest, Japan's. The global balance of military force is witnessing a similar transformation. China's vast wealth is enabling it to mount military deployments that challenge US supremacy in the Pacific and offer strategic lending to nations that the United States frowns upon. But all this is occurring while China is in the midst of a political and economic transformation, experiencing internal turmoil comparable only to that of the Cultural Revolution. These are powerful reminders of the twin axioms of a prudent US diplomacy: Chinese cooperation is essential to a stable global order but military preparedness on the part of the United States and its allies remains the ultimate guarantor of collective security.

China nonetheless provides a fundamental challenge to the United States, one that is not only strategic – like the USSR – but also civilizational. Whether or not China can be integrated and coexist peacefully in a global order not of its own making remains the great imponderable. The Soviet Union was a peer military threat but its economy was never a serious rival to the United States. China, by contrast, poses the potential to eclipse the United States both economically and militarily. Like great powers previously, increasing economic heft has translated into burgeoning military power. But the military remains firmly under the control of the Communist Party, whose priority is to cling to power through a combination of economic success and appeals to Chinese nationalism, communism itself having long lost any remnant of popular legitimacy. For the party leaders, much as for Putin in Russia, their animating fear is less external (despite the appeals to anti-Americanism and xenophobia to deflect from problems at home) than internal: a crisis or popular uprising leading to a challenge to the regime.

Such a context provides ominous warnings. After all, although American entry into World War II is dated from December 7, 1941, the Japanese had laid the groundwork for war long before the Pearl Harbor attack. The surprise raid merely made Americans aware of a conflict that had, in Japanese eyes, already commenced. Although John Updike had anticipated a nuclear war between the United States and China in 2020 in his 1997 novel *Toward the End of Time*,[27] the popularity in Washington of the summer 2015 "must-read" novel, *Ghost Fleet*, was testimony to growing American fears of China's rise. Subtitled *A*

Novel of the Next World War, the work dared to imagine the unimaginable, a global war between China and the United States (for those doubtful of the premise, there were endorsements from such heavyweights as retired Admiral James Stavridis, former supreme allied commander of NATO, and D. B. Weiss, executive producer of HBO's *Game of Thrones*)[28]

To pessimists, China represents a modern version of Wilhelmine Germany. While the United States seeks to develop a serious and constructive bilateral relationship, and to assist China's transition to a stable economy, Chinese intentions remain opaque. China stood as the potential engine of growth in the global economy and its policymakers since the 2008 crisis have sought to rebalance the domestic economy away from export-led growth at break-neck speed toward one of greater domestic consumption to meet the needs of the nation's burgeoning urban middle class. For many years, the United States has run a huge external deficit, financed by a surplus of savings from China. Because China's financial system is underdeveloped, and the United States has the world's largest and most liquid government bond market, the flow of funds from China into the US Treasury has effectively allowed American consumers to live beyond the nation's means. But a necessary correction has been occurring as China stimulates domestic demand and American consumers repair their savings. China has also tried to use its economic weight to tilt the balance of influence in the Asia-Pacific in its favor. Its Asian Infrastructure Investment Bank has attracted US allies such as the United Kingdom, Australia and South Korea, as well as Indonesia, India, Malaysia, Myanmar, the Philippines and Singapore. The Regional Comprehensive Economic Partnership – involving ASEAN, Australia, China, India, Japan, New Zealand and South Korea – is widely seen as a rival to the US-led TPP.

To some, though it made sound strategic sense at the time, Nixon and Kissinger's "opening" to China has created a Frankenstein monster for Washington. Growing economic clout has encouraged increasing military assertiveness. Chinese security strategy for decades was based on deterring invasion through a massive but relatively unsophisticated, low-tech military. But with the vast growth of its economy since 1978, Beijing increasingly perceived new opportunities to flex its muscles. Chinese national security and military strategies increasingly embraced power projection and challenging US dominance of the Asia-Pacific.

One expression of this has been the immense qualitative and technological upgrade of China's armed forces, whereby Beijing is pursuing – according to the Pentagon – "a long-term, comprehensive military modernization program" and investing in capabilities to defeat adversary power projection and counter third party intervention during a crisis or conflict[29] On September 3, 2015, the display of *Dongfeng* ("east wind") ballistic missiles in the vast military parade commemorating the seventieth anniversary of victory in World War II was a demonstration of its military might. Named after Mao's slogan that "the east wind will prevail over the west wind," the missiles could potentially sink an aircraft carrier with a single strike. Although Xi announced a reduction of China's armed forces of 300,000 as a testament to Beijing's desire for peace, the public relations pitch was typically deceptive. The cuts were designed to modernize Chinese forces and allow more resources to the navy and air force, the offensive prongs of the regime's efforts to subdue Taiwan and dominate the seas of East and South China. Even after the reduction is implemented, China will retain some 2 million personnel in uniform, almost twice the number as the United States has managed.

A second indication of growing power projection has been the territorial claims and land-grabs pursued with growing assertiveness since 2009. China has added a total of 2,000 acres (800 hectares/8.1 sq km) of the South China Sea to its territory since January 2014. This represents a significant increase compared to the period prior to January 2014, when China reclaimed 12.3 acres (5 hectares/0.05 sq km). The reclamation project has led to China expanding its acreage on the Spratly Islands, in the southern part of the South China Sea, by more than 400 times. With oil rigs and ships in waters claimed by Chinese neighbors and airstrips being constructed on remote specks of islands, Beijing is building a "great wall of sand" in the South China Sea.

A third expression of Beijing's newfound ambition was increasing cooperation with Russia, not just on economic matters of mutual interest (where cooperation has mostly proven glacial) but also on military endeavors, including joint land and sea-based operations. The measures reflected and reinforced a growing projection of naval capacities, in particular. In September 2015, the Chinese even sent warships to the Bering Sea off Alaska while President Obama was visiting the state, the first time China's navy had advanced so close to the US homeland.

A fourth form of Chinese assertiveness is expanded cyber-attacks on the US government and private sector entities. In 2015, this reached new levels with the massive penetration of the Office of Personnel Management's database of security clearance applications. Although the Obama administration publicly stated that it was reviewing its retaliatory options and possible sanctions, no actual responses were implemented. Nonetheless, that the White House had even reached that point was itself indicative of the extent of the increasing threat.

What causes additional anxiety in Washington is the steady accumulation of actions by Beijing. China's publicly declared "One Belt, One Road" strategy is already strengthening ties not only across Southeast Asia but also with key nations bordering the Middle East, such as Pakistan and Afghanistan. More than his predecessors, President Xi Jinping is modeling his leadership on Mao's, assuming a firm hold of the levers of party and state, and demonstrating clearly to domestic and foreign audiences that he intends to speak quietly but stiffen Chinese diplomacy with a big stick that is getting progressively larger each year. Under Xi, his predecessor's slogan of a "quiet rise" has even been replaced by a "Chinese Dream." Whether or not we are approaching the end of American, but are not yet at the beginning of Chinese, world order, Beijing is clearly willing to contemplate at least risking a clash with the United States more than it was in the past.

Russia, too, has taken advantage of apparent American retrenchment to assert its own great power claims much more aggressively. As far back as December 1999, President Putin had outlined his vision of national revival in a "Millennium Message" address that stressed the importance of building a strong state, an efficient economy and developing a distinctive Russian "idea" that together could restore national self-confidence after the humiliation of the USSR's collapse:

Russia has (just) experienced one of the most difficult periods in its many centuries of history … She faces the real danger of becoming not just a second- but even a third-tier country. To prevent this from happening, we need an immense effort from all the nation's intellectual, physical and moral forces.[30]

In the war with Georgia, annexing of Crimea, and "hybrid war" in Ukraine, Putin has tried to deliver on this revanchist platform and appears determined to sustain Russia on a military-driven expansionist path. Approximately 80,000 troops participated in Russian military exercises during the spring of 2015. As the European Leadership Network analysis concluded of Russia's exercise, "Russia is actively preparing for a conflict with NATO, and NATO is preparing for a possible confrontation with Russia."[31] The Russian thrust was both to intimidate NATO and demonstrate to the West that Moscow is prepared to fight for its security, from its neighbors to the future Arctic natural resources bonanza. Making peace for Putin would represent a sapping of virility. The president takes seriously his project for a Eurasian economic union, a multination community that rejects American/Western values, focuses on economic growth and relegates democratic and human rights to a secondary place. Similarly, Putin views Central and Eastern Europe as condemned by geography to enjoying only limited sovereignty and best functioning under strong, rather than democratic, leaders. Westphalian norms of territorial integrity and the freedom of choice of sovereign nations matter only selectively. Moreover, Putin's ambitions extend well beyond the "post-Soviet space," with Russian military personnel and equipment actively assisting the defense of the Assad regime in Syria from the fall of 2015.

A hollowing out of state power, a rising but anxious China, a revanchist but fragile Russia and an internally discordant United States perhaps together imply that Obama's was the correct choice: accept the arrival of a post-American era, close the final chapter of history's "American Century" and set in train the long-term management of a diminishing role as successfully as feasible. But is this case really as plausible as declinists, realists, offshore balancers and those non-Americans eager for a United States in retreat claim?

The "antideclinist" rejoinder: "deja vu all over again"

Uneasy lies the head that wears the crown, not least when regicidal rivals abound. But, despite the many portentous warning signs at home and abroad, there remains much to the case that the notion of "Peak America" remains premature.[32] Declinist accounts tend to exhibit three features that together limit their analytic purchase: an ahistoricism (neglecting the prior historical precedents for such misplaced arguments, in relation to the Soviet Union during the 1950s/1960s, the European Economic Community of the 1970s, West Germany and Japan in the 1980s and China since the 2000s); an overreaction (to current trends that are extrapolated too deterministically or too far to prove convincing); and a persistent underestimation of the strong fundamentals underpinning US staying power (often animated by a basic antipathy to market capitalism). Declinism has been the avant-garde dog that consistently didn't bark. That doesn't mean that the pooch is incapable of howling long and hard now, but that the precedents point in a more docile direction.

If one steps back from the more fevered analyses to consider the possible dimensions of America's continuing comparative strength, five features loom especially large.

First, despite John Kerry's claim about the existence of global anti-Americanism, the extent of this phenomenon is more broad than deep. Few governments express an active desire to distance themselves from Washington, either publicly or privately. If anything, as the Obama years confirm, allies are disquieted by lack of proximity to US decision making. Even where those allies' populations express antipathy toward – typically – the US president or a specific American foreign policy, mass disapproval also tends to be episodic. Moreover, the real salience of anti-American beliefs to states' actual policies is limited, at best. At the height of opposition to the Iraq War and vehement animus directed at George W. Bush, cooperation on intelligence sharing and counterterrorism continued apace with France, Germany and even Russia. Trade and commerce went on undisturbed. "Anti-American" protestors purchased Nike footwear, New York Yankees baseball caps and frequented the movies to watch the latest Hollywood releases. That is, to the extent that it exists, anti-American sentiment is of very limited political, much less geopolitical, significance. Nor did, or does, it clearly indicate the collapse of American "soft power." As has often been remarked of Arab attitudes to the United States, the operative anti-American posture is "Yankee Go Home (And Take Me With You)!"

Second, too myopic a focus on aggregate GDP statistics is invariably misleading as to the full complement of power that the United States, both absolutely and relative to other states, still retains. Structural accounts of US foreign policy tend to emphasize systemic forces, deep structural explanations, iron laws and constellations of power. American policy has little room for malleability or discretion. Statecraft is rigid rather than plastic, sparing little room for maneuver to domestic whims, pathologies and electoral cycles. America is apparently bereft of options in the face of impersonal forces that are working their way through the international system and wreaking their changes regardless of what others in the West either desire or how they act.

But this is a misleading picture. The United States no longer possesses the 50 percent of global GDP that it did in 1945, nor an economy five times larger than the nearest challengers. But then, neither does it possess the three-fourths of the world's military spending that it enjoyed at that time either. Few critics point to the drop in the latter category as evidence of decline. More importantly, per capita rates of GDP really do point to different countries. China's remains at the level of states such as Ecuador or Serbia and is unlikely to even approach that of the United States for a generation or more.

The more salient fact is that the United States was and remains the only state possessing preponderance in *all* the underlying components of national power: economic, military, technological and geopolitical, with the underrated fallback of inhabiting the safest neighborhood in the world (topography still provides the most rudimentary but powerful comparative advantage to the United States and hugely constrains its main rivals). As Stephen Brooks and William Wohlforth persuasively argue,[33] there exists an important distinction between power as resources and power as results: even at the height of post-1945 power, US dominance was hardly total (in conflicts or during energy crises, the 1970s era of stagflation and so on). Washington could not necessarily translate its impressive national resources into success in discrete cases. But none of that diminished the systemic reality of American power. Similarly, despite specific instances of relative policy failure – Afghanistan, Iraq, the Great Recession – primacy remains intact. Washington retains a unique global array of formal and informal allies, friends and "partners." Its enemies can be named on the fingers of one hand: Russia, Iran, Venezuela, North Korea (and perhaps China). Even these evince occasional cooperation on matters of shared interest. Moreover, despite fitful attempts by Beijing and Moscow at diplomatic innovation, only the United States possesses the capacity genuinely to lead. It has not been an excess of US leadership but a deficit that was problematic under Obama. But like a poker player who is dealt a hand comprising half the deck of cards, even if America plays occasional good hands poorly, it is difficult for the United States to lose the game.

Third, in terms of the *hard power* that – notwithstanding the protestations of those lacking it – remains the true currency of value in international politics, the United States remains formidable and without a true peer competitor. Even without considering the latent power of America – the potential that could be mobilized with the kinds of wartime measures imposed from 1941 to 1945 – there exists formidable strength across military and economic power. Although it is drawing close to a precipice, the primacy of the US military is, for the time being, unparalleled. China's military threat is real and growing, but its capacity to project military power on a global scale remains impaired. Provided the United States attends to restoring its quantitative and qualitative military edge across all dimensions, it will be some years before China can compete globally. Moreover, with the key exceptions of China and Russia, there has been a marked absence of hard "counterbalancing" since 1991. The injection of funds that accrue to Iran from the nuclear deal may tilt the balance in one region, but Tehran poses a limited conventional threat to its neighbors, much less directly to the United States. Indeed, continuing shared threat perceptions about states such as Iran, Russia, China and North Korea (as well as terrorism, chemical, biological, radiological and nuclear weapons, and cyber-warfare) continue to unify, and potentially broaden, the "West."

Even on the dimension where the United States appears most vulnerable, there remains no alternative model competing with market capitalism as there was during the Cold War. The intellectual flirtation with market authoritarianism and a putative "Beijing consensus" that enjoyed adherents for a time in the 2000s has largely been ended by the increasing problems inherent in China's economic management and the drop in oil prices that deprived petro-states such as Russia and Venezuela of substantial leverage. Sharp falls in commodity prices and the failure of the Russian economy to diversify curtailed Moscow's ambitions after 2014. According to official government figures, the Russian economy shrank 46 percent in the second quarter of 2015 while the ruble also weakened sharply against the US dollar. Harmed more by low oil prices than punitive but selective Western sanctions, the Russian economy slipped into recession for only the second time in Putin's fifteen years in power. None of this negates the dangers posed by Moscow. The Kremlin is perennially concerned about mass protests and regional defiance that could result from economic crisis. But it illustrates the limits to the challenge posed by the supposed rise of the BRICS. Where they have succeeded, states such as India and Brazil have seen successes predominantly through liberalization, not posing alternative models. Even economically thriving states such as Germany see leading companies choosing to locate in the United States: the largest BMW plant is in South Carolina.

As such, the economic future is less that of a "post-American" versus an Americanized world but more one of which type of capitalism (those tending to lighter or heavier regulation by government, lesser or greater fiscal responsibility) will prove most productive. Furthermore, in terms of the centrality of the US economy, relatively little has altered. China has ramped up in significance and exerts a powerful sway, but the true engine of global growth remains the United States. And while anticapitalists eagerly anticipated the 2008 financial crisis discrediting capitalism for good, it did not. The distinction between the financial system and global capitalism remained crucial and the appropriate regulation of the former was recognized as a crucial component of the successful operation of the latter. Far from parties of the left ascending, parties of the right have tended to win public favor in managing economic recovery and authoring reform. When it comes to critical aspects of a twenty-first-century economy – flexibility and adaptability, research excellence, productivity, competitiveness, innovation in information technology, nanotechnology and patents – the United States remains in a position that other states can only dream about. Finally, one can factor into all of this the American energy revolution. In 2013–14 alone, while the United States enjoyed a surge of over a million barrels per day in its liquid fuels supply (including crude oil and biofuels), supply from OPEC countries dropped sharply. The United States is on its way to being a net exporter of energy with substantial benefits, potentially, for collective Western security.

That the United States cannot dictate the foreign, economic and energy policies of every major power in the world is obvious. It cannot sanction the world's largest banks or cut off countries like China from the American financial system. As major purchasers of US debt, such actions could trigger severe disruptions in the American economy and raise questions internationally about the dollar's role as the world's reserve currency. That is part of the reason why successive presidents including Clinton, Bush and Obama chose not to employ the punitive third party legislative instruments made available to them by Congress. America's rivals are also clearly interested in the idea of displacing the dollar. The People's Bank of China suggested this as early as 2009 and Russia has been explicit about this goal under Putin, who called in 2014 for the BRICS to develop a system of measures that would help prevent the harassment of countries that do not agree with foreign policy decisions made by the United States and its allies. But the dollar has rarely been as strong as it was over 2014–16. The notion that it could be replaced as a reserve currency is laughable at this point on a geopolitical basis. Alternatives to the dollar as the world's reserve currency are not viable. The euro remains massively dysfunctional and there are few signs that the types of reforms necessary to the EU to make it otherwise are politically acceptable any longer to European electorates. Fluctuations in the renminbi powerfully indicate that it remains far from ready to supplant the dollar. In short, although many states have been hollowed out, the locus of real power remains with the state, and the hard power that shapes international politics remains favorable to the United States and the West.

Fourth, despite the intense and intemperate internal political disagreements over illegal immigration that the Trump presidential campaign reflected and reinforced, America enjoys an enviably high birth rate and a rare capacity to ensure periodic renewal through immigration. According to a 2010 Gallup study, about 24 percent of the world's adults hoping to emigrate listed the United States as their ideal destination – more than three times the number wanting to head to second-placed Canada. The expansionist immigration regime remains intact despite the disconnect with American public opinion because it delivers concrete benefits to a range of powerful proimmigration groups while the costs – often more psychological rather than tangible – are dispersed among an unorganized, albeit large, public for whom issues other than immigration are usually more salient on Election Day. Millions, from

Mexico to the Middle East, daily risk their lives to reach America and Europe – not, in Langston Hughes' words, "toward the warmth of other suns" in China, Russia or India.

Fifth and finally, there is a simple but profound question of who exactly is placed to assume the mantle of global leadership if the declinists are correct about America's rise and fall. Niall Ferguson was surely right to argue, over a decade ago, that the US role in maintaining a "liberal empire" is impeded by three key deficits of budget, manpower and attention (after Iraq, Ferguson added a fourth, legitimacy).[34] But Paul Kennedy argued that the key to the British Empire rested on the basic refusal of other nations to spend the time or energy to challenge the British. The question arises as to whether this has really altered for the United States as it heads into the 2020s. With the possible exceptions of Russia, Iran and China, do other states seriously covet America's leading role or do they recognize that they cannot solve regional and global challenges without the United States – still the "indispensable" nation even if it's no longer the "inescapable" one?

Among its neighbors and the recipients of its investment, there remain remarkably few takers for the arrival of a Sinocentric world order. At least as important, Beijing faces multiple internal strains from strikes and industrial unrest to environmental decay and a skewed demography (formally shifting its one-child to a two-child family policy in 2015). China's economy continues to slow, across a broad range of indicators: industrial production, real estate investment and retail sales, a key measure of household consumption. Shares in China took a steep fall – literally and figuratively – in 2015–16, as signs of a substantial slowdown became increasingly apparent. China's central bank allowed the renminbi to fall. Having appreciated against the dollar and yen, the Chinese responded to Western pressure to allow market forces to prevail. When it went too far, Beijing spent approximately $200 billion to prop it up. Policies have been ineffective and inconsistent, with attempts to boost China's flagging exports among numerous measures to address the nation's broader economic turbulence. Such moves to boost its economic growth, often accompanied by protectionist measures, often harm American companies and inflame an inter-mittently heated debate in the United States about whether China is stealing middle-class jobs. A weaker currency makes US goods exported to China more expensive and Chinese goods exported abroad relatively cheap, weighing on sales of American companies, from well-known brands such as Apple to thou-sands of smaller companies, threatening to slow the US economic recovery.

But again, America has options when it comes to its bilateral relationships. In the Chinese instance, Washington could make concessions to Beijing to establish some kind of G-2 power-sharing construct. Whether this would sat-isfy Chinese players, themselves divided, and work in practice, is questionable (it is sometimes remarked that either Beijing or Washington can dominate the Asian region but not both). Or the United States could pursue counterpres-sure. In asymmetric form this might suggest downgrading or ending military cooperation, taking economic steps, including sanctions, or developing US military capabilities for irregular warfare. More symmetric, direct measures could involve expansion of power projection and naval capabilities, enhanced cyber-capabilities and more closely integrated and even formalized military alliances.

In sum, in terms of viable alternatives to Washington, all the putative competitors for leading the global order face serious internal and external security challenges, flattening or falling populations, shrinking labor forces and ageing populations (by 2050, the median German age will be fifty-two, while America's will be forty-one). One perhaps need not go so far as some do, claiming that the combination of global ageing and nuclear weapons among the great powers is yielding a "geriatric peace" to last. Even with the ageing of its people and the slowing of China's growth, the nation will continue to exert seismic effects on the global system. Yet China possesses the material capacity but not the political legitimacy to lead and its internal problems constantly threaten the integrity of the state. Russia exhibits the desire to lead but possesses neither the material capacity nor the political legitimacy. The possible collapse of the Russian state looms as a very real future possibility. As for the EU, despite its convulsions over the euro, the material capacity of the Union affords it the wherewithal to lead. But the EU has neither the political capacity nor the will. The chronic pressures of internal division, demography, immigration, vulnerability to Russia and enduring military weakness make it a "postmodern" but distinctly un-paradise-like continent. If America is not to lead, there are no viable alternatives for restoring world order.

Conclusion

Whatever the relative failures of his presidency, the United States can and should take justified pride in the historic election and reelection of Barack Obama. To some, that verdict may too closely resemble the apocryphal query, "apart from that, Mrs Lincoln, how did you enjoy the show?" But, for all of the problems that undoubtedly fester, and the noisy nativist voices that object, the United States remains by some margin the most successful, vibrant and inclusive multiracial, multiethnic and religiously tolerant nation on earth. Its liberal culture typically tempers and trumps zealotry at home and, abroad, offers a standing rebuke to the authoritarian conformity, the suppression of dissenting voices and looks, and the outright repression of Russia, China, Iran, North Korea and other revisionist states. In 2015, the United States legalized same sex marriage nationwide and states across the South confronted their racial histories and removed Confederate battle flags across the region. Can the Russians, Chinese, Iranians and others credibly offer similar comparisons to confronting the darker aspects of their pasts – and indeed, their present – as directly? Is a politician of color a serious prospect for president or prime minister in any European state?

Moreover, to the extent it impacts international affairs, and for all the alleged anti-Americanism out there, global "soft power" is still dominated by the West, with the United States ranking third in a leading global influence index in 2015, while China was ranked at the very bottom (so much for the profusion of Confucius Institutes).[35] A mostly Western-authored technological revolution is currently underwriting the greatest advances in human welfare in history. The scale of progress is astonishing. From the impact of mobile phone technology in developing nations, GM crops on food security or shale's role in forcing down oil prices, capitalist enterprises are driving progressive change. Silicon Valley, through Amazon, Apple, Google and Facebook, has transformed the lives of billions around the globe. Thanks to the abandonment of communism and command economies, the proportion of the world population living in extreme poverty has collapsed from more than half to just over a fifth since the 1980s. Absent a new world war, global inequality should continue to shrink, diseases be cured and the quality of life improve. Ultimately, in time, clean energy should permit all nations to reduce their carbon footprints without crippling their economies with today's expensive but immature renewable technologies. A single American program initiated under George W. Bush – the President's Emergency Plan for AIDS Relief – has saved millions of African lives; no member of the BRICS can boast anything remotely similar. In short, contrary to today's successors to Friedrich Nietzsche, Oswald Spengler and H. G. Wells, the United States and the West have much to be proud of, and to draw on, for the coming struggles.

Although the German historian Leopold von Ranke once wrote that, "Most see their ruin before their eye; but they go on into it," reports of America's demise remain premature. American democracy is a divided one by constitutional design and historical evolution. The body politic is nonetheless hurting and in need of a healing that looks elusive and distant. The Trump phenomenon, complex and multifaceted as it is, represents a symptom of a disgruntled people fearing the fading of the American Dream and an expression of a democracy experiencing a serious crisis of self-confidence. The notion that a rising tide lifts all boats is under strain, and the crisis of the middle class poses a major long-term issue in need of resolution if the American social fabric is to remain solid. But the US order is also stable, secure, peaceful and universally respected and revered. For all the nightly news attention to scenes of division and conflict over guns, religion, race, immigration and more, the US Constitution still provides the shared basis by which Americans can find ways to disagree and resolve their differences. It helps to perpetuate a robust and adaptive civil society, with an unmatched capacity to absorb and Americanize millions of legal and illegal immigrants, and liberal tolerance for peoples of all faiths and none. With perhaps the most enviable geographical location, natural resources in abundance, enormous domestic energy supplies, the largest economy in the world, and the best universities, research institutions and leading innovators in science and technology, the United States occupies a position and possesses material resources that most, if not all, other nations still envy.

But it would be foolish to complacently adopt a Panglossian view of the Lazarus-like United States. Trying to weigh whether America's domestic woes or foreign retreat represent the greater problem is an artificial thought experiment. Both are interrelated. The next US president needs to attend more assiduously to the bully pulpit: to educating, shaping and sustaining public support for American foreign policy, and to offer support, hope and inspiration to those oppressed peoples courageously struggling for their own human rights and representative forms of government. It is difficult in all modern democracies to focus public attentions on international affairs outside crisis conditions. But underplaying the stakes of America's global role is a luxury that the United States cannot afford. In an age where cyber-warfare or EMP attacks can cripple entire economies, there is something deeply complacent about too myopic a focus on domestic woes, no matter how serious. Likewise, a populist appeal for protectionist measures when foreign investment remains a crucial part of sustaining American growth seems calculated more to appeal to raw emotion than dispassionate reason. Moreover, the problem with a strategy of offshore balancing is that while remaining offshore is easy enough to accomplish, it is not commensurate with achieving a genuine balancing in the regions critical to US and global security.

There was a satirical UK program in the late 1970s called *Not the Nine O'Clock News* that once featured a spoof of the BBC's weekly current affairs show *Question Time* (where five leading politicians and public figures are quizzed by a live studio audience). In this instance, the panel was informed that the Soviet Union had just launched 50,000 megatons of nuclear warheads against Britain, which would be arriving in four and a half minutes, and was asked for their views on Britain's future as a world power. While the Conservative Party politician rambled incoherently about Britain not being an island, the left-wing representative offered the observation, "Well, I'm amazed. We're sitting here talking about a nuclear holocaust, casually discussing the destruction of the entire planet, and ignoring the major issue, which is the appalling record of this Conservative government. The real tragedy here is that three million people will die *unemployed*."[36]

Echoes of that perverse prioritization and calcified partisan orthodoxies are not difficult to discern in today's American political debates, as if a binary choice has to be made between either domestic renaissance or foreign engagement. As most Americans recognize, although national resources are not infinite, the fortunes of their nation and the wider world are inextricably linked. The United States can flourish once more at home and abroad. But to do so requires restoring a grand strategy appropriate to the challenges of the world after Obama.

5

The way forward: a new American internationalism

2° NOTES P.137

America is at a strategic crossroads. The post-Obama years offer a simple but profound choice: continue a set of well-intentioned but failed and failing policies that have weakened the United States, the free world and international order, or change course. A strong case commends embracing a new direction based on the confluence of interests and ideals that informed America's rise to global preeminence. And if there exists some irony in recalling the past to guide future direction into the third decade of the twenty-first century, that is only appropriate. Reverence for the wisdom of the framers of the US Constitution – flawed as they were – and the values underpinning constitutional democracy still strongly informs domestic political debates. A return to an effectively enlightened foreign policy tradition – flawed in execution as it sometimes was – seems equally judicious at this critical juncture.

In the looming choice over the future of US statecraft, there are echoes of 1980, when Americans had the opportunity to confirm a failed strategy by reelecting Jimmy Carter as president or embark on a more assertive path under Ronald Reagan. But, if anything, the contemporary challenge is even more momentous. In 1980, the bipolar structure of international relations seemed entrenched; even Reagan was not bold enough to predict the beginning of the Cold War's final days on his watch. By contrast, global politics are now more unstable than at any time since the 1930s. The stakes are as high as the outcomes are uncertain. The terminal prospect of world order collapsing and an unstable multipolarity, or even a chaotic a-polarity, emerging is very real. The next president will craft relations with a world in flux until 2021 or 2025, a period that could prove as consequential for US power and prosperity as any since 1945. Much more than merely ratifying retrenchment and retreat, or recrafting the policies that made America a global power without precedent, hangs in the balance.

Like Carter in his final year, Obama too quietly acknowledged the error of his ways by latterly modifying his approach in 2015–16, breaking his own "redlines" (keeping 9,880 troops through 2016 in Afghanistan and 5,500 into 2017, sending troops to Iraq and special operations forces into Syria). But for some, such as Barry Posen and Ian Bremmer, "leading from behind" has not retreated far enough. The world is becoming smaller, and so should America. Posen advocates an unapologetic strategy of offshore balancing, or "restraint.①" Bremmer outlines three options②First, "independence": without endless blood and treasure to spend on others, the United States will fare better by devoting its energies and resources to rebuilding strength from within. Second, a "moneyball" America: Washington cannot afford every fight to support liberal values but must defend national interests wherever they are threatened, albeit subject to America's limitations. Third, "indispensable" America: operating autonomously is not only foolish but dangerous, since the world relies on US leadership and America has interests requiring active involvement abroad. Although weighing the respective arguments carefully, Bremmer makes a plain preference for an "independence" that, despite his denial, closely resembles neo-isolationism and a plaintive call to "come home, America."

But three ironies undermine accounts advocating even greater disengagement. First, as a prescriptive matter, the Obama administration had already tried out the independent and moneyball scripts for size. We have seen what emerges both for global order (its steady breakdown) and America (diminished influence, fractured alliances and the ascent of adversaries). Second, although critics favoring disengagement pose as internationalists and regard Obama as "Bush-lite" – maintaining excessive continuity with Bush era "militarism" and "unilateralism" – they advocate policies that are at once nationalist and unilateral in the extreme. Nothing could be less internationalist and more singular than retreating from active involvement abroad regardless of the views of, and consequences for, others (never mind the long-term results for America). Third, although they imply otherwise, the entirely appropriate focus on economic foundations advocated by neo-isolationism's apologists need not impede investing adequately in the necessary diplomatic, military and other actions to bolster US power abroad③America can walk and chew gum at the same time, standing tall in the process.

Taking the off-ramp from global leadership may nonetheless tempt many Americans. Gas prices seem unaffected by Sunnis and Shias slaughtering each other, Jews and Christians across the Middle East, Asia and Africa. Importing cheap consumer durables from Asia continues, undisturbed by diplomatic spats over uninhabited islands, cyber theft of US intellectual property and Beijing's growing inventory of anti-ship missiles. Parochial internal European squabbles over the sclerotic euro, Greek bailouts and destabilizing refugee crises make Mediterranean vacations cheaper. And Moscow's corruption, gangsterism and repression of LGBT Russians, dissidents and democracy activists have minimal play in Peoria. Justifying coercive diplomacy, enhanced defense spending or military action to Americans preoccupied by domestic concerns like jobs and immigration "because of a quarrel in a faraway country between people of whom we know nothing" can appear needlessly provocative, unappealing and even counterproductive. Meeting challenges judiciously rather than taking an active role in solving global problems is more attractive. With a growing economy, surging energy production, declining exports and the security of occupying the most stable corner of the globe, a self-reliant America can insulate itself against possible crises. While the new normal of a more restrained US global role will make the world even less predictable, other countries can adjust. Perhaps there is a cold but compellingly mature logic to the Obama policy to, as one State Department official put it, "let the world graze its knees and learn that Uncle Sam won't come running every time" ⟨4⟩

But that seductive vision, as we learned many decades ago when Neville Chamberlain – a "hard-headed realist" of his era – articulated the very definition of appeasement, is all too myopic and, in the end, self-defeating. From cyber threats to ISIS-inspired terrorism, nuclear proliferation to economic meltdown, America cannot safely isolate itself from the dangerous centripetal forces convulsing the wider world. If anything, an apparently weakening United States makes it even more of an inviting target for those states and non-state actors hostile to Western civilization and the open order it has sustained. Moreover, with the devolution of deadly technology once possessed only by states to the level of a single terrorist cell or malign scientist with a DNA lab in his basement – an Edward Snowden with smallpox samples – no American can prudently afford to be unconcerned by the dark side of global interdependence. As Duff Cooper – a Conservative Cabinet member who resigned in disgust the day after Prime Minister Chamberlain concluded the 1938 Munich Agreement with Hitler for "peace in our time" – trenchantly observed, while "war with honor, peace with dishonor" exists at the margins of acceptability, "war with dishonor" (being forced into fighting after appeasing an enemy had failed) "that was too much." The alluring but jejune notion that US retreat can keep the homeland a sanctuary nation of security in a less benign and more dystopian world has been tested since 2009. The unedifying results of Obama's less-is-more approach are plain to see. Hope alone cannot preclude gathering storm clouds blowing ever closer to American shores and making American lives markedly unquiet.

But, although there exists no Doctrine Deficit – with the exceptions of JFK, LBJ, Gerald Ford and George H. W. Bush, every president since Truman has had an eponymous foreign policy doctrine – effective grand strategies are more easily desired than designed and delivered. The complexity of contemporary global challenges do not allow for a single overarching concept comparable to containment to sustain a Truman Doctrine 2.0 for the early twenty-first century. The Herculean foreign policy problems confronting the forty-fifth president will be even more complex than previously. In cleaning the Augean stables after Obama, the next commander in chief will be dogged by the twin "fogs" of policy and war, with neither the time for on-the-job training nor the luxury of making the perfect the enemy of the good on Russia, China, Iran, ISIS and still other dilemmas yet to emerge. But if America chooses to move beyond being a global bystander, a new strategy to maximize the nation's core interests needs calibrating – one that is serious about adversaries, mindful of the limits of engagement, averse to politicizing national security and geared to delivering the possible and affordable. In navigating the new world disorder, the touch-stones of a revised approach rely on a resumption of core elements underpinning pre-Obama foreign policy. Abroad, that means proactively shaping global events, not merely reacting to them, through judiciously crafting counterforce and methodically advancing "strategies of pressure."(5)At home, it demands a dedicated leadership that addresses the American people with clarity. Needless to add, it will also have to overcome – since it cannot plausibly transcend – the envenoming of US politics that has been broadening and deepening for four decades.

Others will author their own nomenclature for a strategy seeking to coherently integrate interests, threats, resources and policies, but one way to frame it is as a New American Internationalism. The residual problems left by the forty-fourth president will take years to remedy and may well worsen before they improve. But the approach outlined here can at least begin the process of reversing the losses of the Obama era, renewing US leadership and paving a path to ultimately restoring global order.

A post-Obama Doctrine

E. L. Doctorow claimed that, "Writing is like driving at night in the fog. You can only see as far as your headlights, but you can make the whole trip that way." Unfortunately, crafting an intellectually coherent and effective strategy for a world in disorder is less safely founded on circumspect vision and constant improvisation. After Obama, America needs a more far-sighted, stable approach than erratically driving blind on a road to perdition. Strategy demands a new lodestar, more astringent approach and proper execution. The unrealistic assumptions and unsafe beliefs of the Obama Doctrine should be abandoned. In their stead, a hard-headed assessment of US adversaries should form the basis for strategic resolve; all else is embellishment and detail. Passivity, a "kick the can down the road" approach and threat deflation – awaiting the day when Russia, China and Iran become responsible credits to their great power status – offer no strategy to preclude future days of infamy.

Rebuilding national security and defense

President Obama took an unprecedented axe to the *Pax Americana*. But while US alliances suffered serious wounds, the Pentagon received the sharpest and deepest cut: 1 trillion dollars over ten years. Critics invariably note that the United States maintains the largest defense budget in the world, greater than that of the next ten largest spenders combined (though, measured as a share of GDP, Yemen and Algeria spent more on defense in 2014 than the United States; proportionately, eight of the top fifteen spenders are in the Middle East and North Africa). But numbers alone, like aggregate GDP figures, are a reliable signal neither of intent nor capability, especially with America's military smaller than it was on 9/11 and its qualitative edge eroding. Downsizing the military while threats rise is a reckless gambit.

Ramping up defense is not a sufficient condition of restoring US power and influence. But it is a necessary one. The alternative is that cuts in force structure compel the armed services to inform the next president that they cannot accomplish the tasks for which they are charged. For either party to permit such an eventuality would represent a criminal abnegation of the national interest, not least with 101 military veterans serving as lawmakers in the 114th Congress. To regain lost influence and renew a credible deterrence and forward defense necessitates adequate funding, beyond the $40 billion increase approved in 2015. Moreover, development projects cannot continue to be designed based on the assumption of extensive geopolitical slack and a permissive future threat environment. Instead, the United States needs to prepare for a future where it will have to face militaries like China's on more-or-less equal terms as well as unremitting state and criminal cyber-attacks and asymmetric threats from the likes of ISIS and al Qaeda.

Politically, this is no easy sell. Even now, the gravity of security challenges is widely underestimated. Moreover, planning remains plagued by bureaucratic and intramilitary in-fighting. Pentagon spending is notoriously pork-prone and opaque while aspects of the budget – not least payroll and benefits – require serious reform. But it is worth contextualizing these expenditures. Approximately 97 percent of America's finances are devoted to matters other than national defense. While the defense budget is approximately $650 billion annually, Americans spend $165 billion per year on food waste (40 percent of food in the United States goes uneaten. Interest payments on the national debt are projected by the Congressional Budget Office to overtake defense spending in the early 2020s, reaching 14 percent of the budget by 2024 (compared to 12 percent for defense). Without entitlement reform, America will face insolvency. But without sufficient defense spending, it may face crippling attack. A robust defense is something that most Americans can concur is a proper role for the federal government, not least when threats to national security are rising, not receding.

What does that mean in the context of the contemporary threat environment? In the summer of 2015, senior US military personnel testified – contrary to the civilian leadership of the Obama administration – that Russia represented America's top security threat. Others accorded that status to jihadists. Whether these, China, or others constitute the severest challenge, if future conflicts arrive more rapidly than since 9/11, the importance of the military achieving greater readiness and modernization before the onset of hostilities will only grow. And if, as seems inevitable, such conflicts are likely to prove more technically challenging, the need to invest substantially more in military research and development than today will similarly increase in urgency. Given what we now know about the threats to the United States and its European, Asian and Middle Eastern allies, a reasonably prudent medium-term plan would seek to raise spending – to finance weapons systems, research and development, modernization and procurement – to somewhere between 4 and 5 percent of GDP. "Full spectrum dominance" may be an outdated concept beyond current feasibility but the United States needs to aim for funding commensurate with confronting multiple challenges, even in the knowledge that partisan polarization and fiscal constraints together preclude its complete realization.

Numbers alone are insufficient. But the fact remains that quantity has a quality all its own. The military lacks sufficient size and is neither positioned nor prepared to meet the challenges identified by the Obama administration's own National Military Strategy (NMS) of 2015. The Pentagon is gambling at the higher end of manageable risk in its ability to execute even existing defense strategy. Protecting core national security interests requires anticipating a range of large-scale ground operations if deterrence fails (and in cases of counterinsurgencies, peace enforcement and relief missions), not placing all America's strategic eggs in the baskets of high technology air, sea and cyber operations, robotics, space and special forces. But the Obama administration's 2012 Defense Strategic Guidance and 2014 Quadrennial Defense Review mandated that the military no longer be sized for large-scale stabilization operations. The army will be cut by 40,000 troops over 2015–17 to – in the rosiest scenario – 450,000 active duty soldiers, the minimum necessary to implement current commitments. But reductions may extend further, to as few as 420,000 soldiers in 30 combat brigades, smaller than the armies of China, India and North Korea. That would still leave it as the world's most important military force but 20 percent smaller than when Obama became its commander in chief. Crucially, readiness will have deteriorated to a point where it cannot provide sufficient combat-ready soldiers in the event of an unexpected conflict. An army of 450,000–500,000 troops and Marine Corps of some 200,000 should instead be a baseline target for the next administration and 115th Congress.

The cumulative effect of budget shortfalls has also forced the navy to accept substantial risk, most notably if the military is confronted with a technologically advanced adversary or forced to deny the objective of an opportunistic aggressor in a second region while engaged in an existing major contingency. The 2014 National Defense Panel, a bipartisan, congressionally chartered group of experts, recommended a target force of 323–46 ships. Remedying the effects of sequestration is again necessary to reduce deployment lengths and return the navy to appropriate readiness levels. Without this, the United States will risk repeating having no aircraft carriers deployed to critical areas like the Persian Gulf for a period of months, a symptom of extended deployments that exhaust the readiness of ships and crews.

The $40 billion increase in the 114th Congress' 2015 budget agreement was an important, if modest and very late, start. But budgetary reversals need to encompass not only manpower and platforms but also forward deployments. During his June 2015 European visit, Secretary of Defense Ashton Carter announced that the United States would temporarily stage one armored brigade combat team's vehicles and associated equipment in Central and Eastern European nations. But temporary rotational forces can at best complement, not substitute, an enduring forward deployed presence. Permanently stationed brigades and material represent force multipliers that rotations cannot match. In light of the fundamentally transformed European security environment, the United States should permanently deploy troops to help dissuade Russian aggression against NATO allies.

Similarly, in the Middle East theater – unless Russia eclipses Washington as the ally of choice for Baghdad – US troops need to be embedded with the Iraqi Security Forces (ISF) down to the battalion level, not just at higher echelons. Partnering US troops with Iraqi units in this way was instrumental in bolstering the effectiveness of ISF units a decade ago, and incorporating advisers into Iraqi battalions would likely have a similar effect today. Embedding forward air controllers with Iraqi ground forces would substantially increase the ability of airstrikes to hit targets on the ground. The 2015 air campaign averaged just twelve strike sorties per day, in contrast to Operation Desert Storm in 1991 (1,241), Operation Allied Force in Kosovo in 1999 (298), Operation Iraqi Freedom in 2003 (691) and Operation Enduring Freedom in Afghanistan in 2001 (86). While the Air Force is arguably in less dire straits than companion services, renewed investment in state-of-the-art technology so that fighters such as the F-35 are adequately configured on time is essential for a twenty-first-century force. So, too, is renewed investment in bombers and reversing the decline of the air fleet. A fleet of some 2,500 operationally ready aircraft should be the goal.

In the sixth-century BC, Sun Tzu advised that "the supreme art of war is to subdue the enemy without fighting." If the US plans to recover the credibility it has lost because of the persistent weakness of its foreign policy since 2009, the starting point is rebuilding the military, whose strength helps both to prevent war and achieve victory if conflict is unavoidable. Defense policy invariably prepares for anticipated attacks but rational adversaries in turn adopt strategies and tactics that go unforeseen. Retrenchment strategies falsely suggest a holiday from "black swans" that historically surprise and discombobulate US plans. A disengaged America is instead liable to be more exposed to greater vulnerability and invite shocks. Planning for potential conflicts does not entail anticipating full-scale wars against implausible enemies. But US defenses need to be configured adequately for state and nonstate antagonists, obvious and less transparent contingencies.

Finally, Washington needs to abandon well-meaning but naïve moves toward "global zero." While it is entirely right to encourage negotiated reductions in the nuclear arsenals of the great powers, and essential to share advanced technology to prevent weapons from accidental detonation or capture by terrorists, a more uncertain and turbulent era is hardly the optimal time for disarmament. As Churchill warned in his final address to the US Congress, "Be careful above all things not to let go of the atomic weapon until you are sure, and more than sure, that other means of preserving peace are in your hands." As awful as nuclear weapons are, there exists no superior means of preserving peace and order.

But repaired alliances would help.

Restoring alliance management

Politics is inherently about coalitions. Vital as the possession of a peerless military remains to national security, the value of alliances represents Washington's supreme strategic asset. Historically without precedent, it distinguishes America from its adversaries and forms the bedrock of effective grand strategy. The latter is not simply about what the United States does but as much about allies, clients, potential partners, "frenemies," enemies and the mass of states and peoples that could opt either way.

National interest guides all states' foreign policies. But no great power has ever maintained such a worldwide network of formal and informal alliances for so long as America, encompassing most major economies and democracies. Yet few presidencies have evinced such an inverse relationship between the rhetorical emphasis accorded engagement, diplomacy and partnerships and the benign neglect of core relationships as that of Obama – for whom losing clients abroad appeared an acceptable price for building a client state at home. The lack of leadership has shocked even those Europeans who initially found his inclusive approach so attractive. Examples abound, from early slights over missile defense to Poland and the Czech Republic through the "friendly fire" directed at Israel to the inept diplomacy that ensured it took until July 2015 for Turkey to agree to the United States using its Incirlik airbase to attack ISIS in Syria (only to discover this more a pretext for Turkish attacks on Kurdish separatists than Islamists). Whether or not this neglect amounted to a strategic "conscious uncoupling" or mistaken tactics is unclear. But, as Robert Gilpin has argued, "Retrenchment by its very nature is an indication of relative weakness and declining power, and thus retrenchment can have a deteriorating effect on relations with allies and rivals." The more that allies are treated as "extras" on the world stage rather than actors in their own right, the fewer US leadership options will remain. And the more Washington disengages from allies to focus on accommodating adversaries, the more America will end up with stronger adversaries and fewer, and more bewildered and apoplectic, allies.

It is part of the catechism of US presidents to declare that global problems cannot be resolved by America acting alone, despite in many instances constructing coalitions of convenience rather than necessity. But after Obama, what is required is a recalibration of commitments and rededication to genuine engagement. This is no mere matter of public relations. Without concrete expressions of support, US alliances will decline in number, quality and value, and allies from London to Tokyo may pursue increasingly independent paths that do not chime with American interests. Genuine allies act from conviction, not convenience. Inadequate responses from Washington risk serial misunderstandings and deterrence failure. Moreover, regions and hemispheres are not isolated. Chronic instability and protracted crisis in the Greater Middle East, for example, destabilizes Europe, threatening the Atlantic Alliance while empowering Russia and emboldening China. Prospectively, Washington needs to bring to a close the era of America the Undependable.

Asia

No one doubts that the US-China bilateral is the most important relationship of the twenty-first century. China's ascendance is less a problem to be resolved than a condition to be managed. As such, a demonstration of US commitment to the Asian region is entirely appropriate. In particular, Washington must decide what to do about Chinese efforts to advance an alternative security architecture that affords Beijing increased influence in the region and diminishes the US role. This requires a clear assessment of China's strategic goals, the implications of increased Chinese influence vis-à-vis America's in the Asia-Pacific, and a clear willingness to push back. The TPP agreement, if ratified, will help solidify economic ties. But the United States has no responsible option but to reinforce its regional alliances, nurture and strengthen those states directly affected by Beijing's behavior and give effect to these through its own military deployments and economic diplomacy. As one of Obama's own senior officials recommended, "the US needs to maintain its forward deployment, superior military forces and technological edge, its economic strength and engagement with the region, its alliances, and its enhanced relationships with other emerging powers."[10]

The problem with strategic reassurance was less the concept than the execution, which erred too far toward reassuring China and dissuading allies from actions rather than the reverse. Even the Obama administration belatedly recognized its own naivety in this regard. The 2011 NMS saw a bright future for "a positive, cooperative, and comprehensive relationship with China that welcomes it to take on a responsible leadership role."[11] But the 2015 report instead placed China squarely in the camp of revisionist states seeking to upturn established international order. The astonishing pace of construction in the South China Sea caused Southeast Asian nations to be increasingly worried that the PRC's new capabilities will facilitate *de facto* Chinese control of the surrounding waters. While some might regard the rival claims to various uninhabited islands as the equivalent of "two bald men fighting over a comb" (as Jorge Luis Borges described Argentina's 1982 conflict with the UK over the Falkland Islands), the 2015 strategy expressed particular concern about Beijing's illegitimate claims "to nearly the entire South China Sea."[12] Although such conflicts represent no direct threat to the United States, more than $5 trillion worth of international trade, from Middle East oil headed for Asian markets to children's toys bound for US stores, transits the South China Sea every year. If China can restrict the passage of ships through international waters, that could cause shockwaves for the world economy. The United States needs to make clear to China that Washington rejects its territorial claims and will not acquiesce in unilateral acts that restrict the rights and freedoms of the international community. By not doing so, Washington is tacitly accepting destabilizing moves that are viewed by regional allies – Japan, Vietnam and the Philippines in particular – as highly threatening.

The "pivot" to Asia merits revisiting and implementing properly, but with a renewed emphasis on reassuring allies while deterring – even if Beijing reads that as "containing" – China. Whether obliquely or otherwise, the Obama administration tended to interpret the much-ballyhooed interdependence of US-China relations as somehow constraining Washington more than Beijing. A sensible recalibration would recognize that, for the sake of all parties concerned, China should not misperceive US commitments. To that end, the United States should extend and upgrade its military resources, investments and security support – from aircraft carrier group presence to ballistic missile defenses – more fully. But America possessed naval mastery after the Soviet collapse in 1991 and its forces since then have emphasized carriers, defended closely by submarines and destroyers. Cumulatively these are a concentrated target for China's militarily advanced arsenal. The United States also needs urgently to look to a new generation of naval deployments that are lighter and more widely dispersed.

Washington can also do more to shore up defense cooperation, not only with but between allies, including South Korea, Japan, Indonesia, the Philippines, Australia and India. Although the US-Japan alliance has had its problems, it remains a fulcrum of the projection of US regional power. To its credit, under Ash Carter, the Obama administration began to rewrite the rules for cooperation on issues such as missile defense, cyber and collective self-defense. The update of the "Guidelines for US-Japan Defense Cooperation" takes into account Japan's recent reinterpretation of its constitution and new national security legislation that allow the nation to more aggressively use its armed forces. The change represents the most marked shift in Tokyo's defense posture since World War II. It can and should serve as a model for wider US bilateral relations with allies across East and South Asia.

In addition, the United States should actively encourage greater security cooperation between its allies. It can play a positive role by more closely integrating material and strategy. On the former, new basing and access arrangements for US forces, greater cooperation on defense (including arms sales, research and development, and military exchanges and exercises), and increased allocation of resources to theater would be a positive signal to allies. On the latter, existing bilateral relations can usefully be supplemented by regional institutions that can enhance regular consultation and cooperation among America's partners.

New configurations in Asian geopolitics offer opportunities here. The Indo-Pacific has emerged as a critical regional space for India and China, and Indian Prime Minister Narendra Modi has reached out to Japan and Australia to forge a nascent trilateral partnership. Although this has stoked suspicion in China, Washington should encourage its development. The three regional powers have become more proactive than in the past in managing increasing turbulence in the region caused by Chinese assertiveness. Navies from the United States, India, Japan and Australia collaborated in tsunami relief operations across the Indian Ocean in late 2004. Since then, institutionalized trilateral strategic dialogues have been established between the United States, Japan and Australia; the United States, India and Japan; and India, Japan and Australia. There is no reason that these cannot be transformed into a "quadrilateral" of democratic partners that can cooperate closely across the Indo-Pacific.

It is well known that although many Asian nations are animated by dual fears of Chinese power and intentions, on the one hand, and US disengagement, on the other, their primary concern is being forced to choose between Beijing and Washington. The United States needs to assuage its allies' fears but the Obama era has caused several to hedge against America's inadequate balancing of China's rising power. The passage of the TPP can assist here, by more closely integrating US allies economically but also encouraging a more economically open region outside China. But closer military-to-military ties, institutionalized dialogues – bilateral, trilateral and otherwise – and a stronger US forward presence would be helpful in shaping the recalibration of strategic choices that capitals from Canberra to Tokyo are now contemplating.

Some of the measures that can help in this regard – enhanced missile defenses, improved defense cooperation, new bases and access – ought also to enhance America's forward deterrence against North Korea. The Korean peninsula is experiencing a period of dangerous posturing with substantial risk of escalation and miscalculation. Ultimately, only China can exert substantial pressure on the uniquely dangerous and depraved regime of Kim Jong-Un, and it is no longer clear whether even Beijing can constrain the mercurial dictator. Pyongyang has confounded more US presidents than Havana and the Obama administration's approach proved no better or worse overall than its predecessors in making progress here. There is little that the next administration can do other than strengthen its deterrent posture, work with regional allies, China and Russia to contain North Korea's periodic provocations and prepare for the contingencies of conventional and nuclear attacks and/or regime collapse. Ironically, though, the recklessness of the regime offers an opportunity for Washington to more closely integrate its diplomacy with key East Asian capitals.

It would be premature to view East Asia in the second decade of the twenty-first century as analogous to Europe in the first half of the twentieth and leading, like World War I, to a war no one wanted but no one knew how to stop. But it would also be unwise to discount historical precedents. In 1941,

Japan felt compelled to wage war because Tokyo was convinced that the window of opportunity to challenge the United States militarily, before America had fully recovered from the Great Depression, was closing. The Obama "pivot that wasn't" may have similarly persuaded Beijing that US power in the Asia-Pacific is declining of its own volition and China can fill the growing vacuum with impunity. Washington needs to avoid that misunderstanding by making clear that the United States is committed to remaining the leading Pacific power, even if that occasions disquiet in the Politburo and People's Liberation Army. Equally, if the pessimists are correct, and China is already convinced that conflict is inevitable and preparing accordingly, a more forward-leaning US posture will at minimum permit countermeasures short of war. In order to avoid falling into the Thucydidean trap, the conservative status quo power of the United States needs to expand and consolidate its regional presence and engage seriously in counterforce to constrain the excesses of a rising China.

Europe

Atlanticism is once more under serious strain. Although this began under George W. Bush, it worsened notably under Obama. Inaction on Syria contributed to the largest refugee crisis to confront Europe in seven decades. Russian aggression has fundamentally transformed Europe's security landscape and the United States will have to abandon hope of establishing a constructive relationship with Moscow over the mid-term. Only a robust, forward-leaning policy to revitalize the transatlantic relationship – and create a community resolute in standing up for shared interests and principles – will stave off the Kremlin's malign machinations.

Disengagement and mismanagement have characterized US policy. Historically, NATO's function was, in Lord Ismay's formulation, "to keep the Russians out, the Americans in, and the Germans down." After the end of the Cold War, a "Europe Whole and Free" was the shared objective of the US and European allies, with NATO and EU enlargement together extending Western zones of security and prosperity to the decommunizing east. State sovereignty included the autonomy to adopt political and economic systems. Freedom of choice, along with long-term prosperity and stability, was only possible absent a strategic ambiguity in which neighboring powers – i.e. Russia – could compromise their sovereignty. But Washington underestimated the time frame for democratic institutions to institutionalize and civil society to flourish after decades of oppressive rule. NATO and EU enlargement were important but insufficient to transform Communist countries into strong rule-of-law liberal democracies with open, well-functioning market economies.

Moreover, until 2014, "Europe" was widely assumed to be a settled strategic matter. The Obama administration's Asian pivot was widely interpreted as downgrading Europe as a priority. Part of this entailed the relentless decline of America's military presence. According to official Pentagon figures, US forces fell from 341,000 troops permanently stationed in Europe in 1989 to 118,000 in 2001. While reductions were prudent in the wake of the Soviet Union's disintegration, withdrawals continued to the point where now only 65,000 troops remain. The increasing vulnerability created by the resulting vacuum proved an enticing opportunity for Putin. Russia invaded Georgia in 2008, annexed Crimea and instigated a "hybrid" war on Ukraine in 2014, destabilized neighboring states by cyber-attacks and energy cut-offs, ignited ethnic tensions among Russian-speakers, issued military threats and began funding illiberal parties and NGOs throughout Europe.

Since Crimea's annexation in February 2014, Putin has been on the offense, brazenly and systematically dismantling a major European state in Ukraine while blaming Kiev for aggression, like the murderer who blames the victim for being home when he was burglarizing the victim's house. The Ukraine conflict is ultimately one between competing geopolitical imperatives: Russia's, to protect its interior by using neighboring states to provide a buffer zone, and America's, to preclude the rise of regional powers potentially challenging US hegemony. These collided in the most strategically important former Soviet state for Moscow, whose fate shapes whether or not Russia is a rising regional power or increasingly isolated and vulnerable from within and without by pro-Western forces.

Putin's main advantage has been acting decisively in a script crafted straight from Clausewitz while NATO hesitates. Article V commits the United States to collective defense but Russian nuclear doctrine and "hybrid war" together seek to cause American allies to doubt that NATO would risk military conflict, let alone nuclear war, over the destabilization of a member state. With almost no tactical nuclear weapons left in Europe, the only options would be suicide or surrender. But nothing incites Russian aggression as reliably as signaling lack of resolve. As Matthew Kroenig notes, "NATO must guard against intensifying the arms race – but it would be inaccurate to charge that it risks starting one. An arms race is already under way; NATO is just sitting it out."[13] The West cannot return to "business as usual" with Russia. But there are six steps that Washington can take to avoid playing Russian roulette with a fully loaded chamber.

First, Russia needs to be viewed through neither blindfolds nor rose-tinted lenses. Sensitivity to Russian interests is appropriate. But Moscow is no longer a superpower nor a strategic partner. It is a troubled nation in dire straits with distinct interests promoting an anti-Western value system and intent upon an expansionism far more forceful than American democracy promotion ever managed. As a "sniper-power" that can frustrate the United States but not overcome its influence, a pragmatic and evidence-based approach can calibrate accordingly. Genuine Russian moves toward conciliation – withdrawing from Ukraine and Crimea – should be matched by Washington in full. But insurgency, invasion and expansion equally merit counterforce.

Second, NATO needs reviving. In addition to stationing two or more US combat brigades – about 8,000 troops – in Eastern Europe, conventional deterrent capabilities should be restored as a matter of urgency. Article V requires more than rhetorical reassurance. It compels plans for putting in place substantial, well-armed and well-trained forces for deterrence. NATO must restore its credibility as a deterrent to aggression and demonstrate that limited war is impossible. It also needs to make plain to Moscow that the response to "hybrid" or "ambiguous" war will be robust and immediate. New and permanent forces – ground and air based – merit establishment, alongside enhanced missile, ground, air and cyber defenses. NATO's eastern flank requires urgent upgrading as the key alliance priority.

As part of this, an increased US defense budget should encourage officials to pressure European governments to spend more on defense commensurate with the threat to their security. The United States provides 70 percent of NATO defense spending but cannot, should not and will not meet European challenges alone. The four largest contributors to the alliance – the United States, France, Germany and the UK – cut their defense budgets in 2014 (adjusting for inflation). Nine Eastern European nations increased theirs, with Poland and the Baltic states making substantial investments. Yet overall spending by the twenty-eight member states fell by $50 billion, or 5.3 percent, despite an agreement in principle that all should spend at least 2 percent of their national income on defense. The United States needs to exert real pressure on Europeans to change course, unsuccessful as this has proven previously. Moreover, routinized and effective channels for crisis management between NATO's nuclear powers – the United States, UK and France – urgently need to be institutionalized to avoid repetition of the deterrence fiasco of Syria in 2013.

Third, while Ukraine is not a NATO member and admission currently would be imprudent, Kiev's fate will signal whether victims of Russian aggression can expect real support from the democratic West. The Ukraine Freedom Support Act of 2014 authorized the provision of anti-armor weapons, counterartillery radars and other equipment to aid Ukraine in its fight against Russian-backed separatist rebels. In 2015, the House and Senate included provisions in the FY 2016 National Defense Authorization Act to provide additional funding for this effort. Only Obama's refusal to utilize these instruments stood in the way of firmer support for Kiev. The next president can remove that obstacle, assuming there is still time to save Ukraine. Military assistance, including anti-tank and anti-aircraft weaponry, joint exercises, training and intelligence cooperation should be provided.

Fourth, new candidates can be fast-tracked for membership. Under Obama, progress stalled on expansion efforts (for Macedonia, Montenegro and Georgia). Unexpectedly, the nations that may have the strongest interest in joining NATO are ones that declined to do so during the Cold War: Finland and Sweden. In light of numerous Russian military incursions into their sovereign waters and air space, the Finnish and Swedish publics have expressed growing approval of membership. Washington should fast-track this and cease apologizing for NATO enlargement, a development not imposed but freely chosen by sovereign democracies, and one that has brought unparalleled security and prosperity to Central and Eastern Europe.

Fifth, the United States needs to engage in strategic jujitsu and flip the Russian nationalist card against Putin. Notwithstanding his bluster, Putin is deeply insecure. This is why democratic reformers are murdered in broad daylight or suddenly take ill without explanation. Putin exploits control of the media to promote a xenophobic authoritarian nationalism while hiding his covert war in Ukraine from ordinary Russians. Robust public support for the regime may prove shallow and brittle if confronted by unpleasant realities. Russia may be but a pale shadow of the Soviet Union but the United States can and should engage in another generational battle of ideas to inform Russians about the realities of Putin's corrupt, brutal and kleptocratic rule. Putin uses Russian nationalism and anti-Americanism to distract from an ailing society and declining economy. Russians should learn that their great nation is betrayed and profoundly ill-served by Putinism.

Finally, Washington needs to restore the vision of a Europe whole and free. That vision cannot be realized until every European democracy has the opportunity to seek security through membership in either the EU or NATO or both. Any other course suggests a policy of expediency, content to allow fourteen former Soviet states to remain subordinate to Russia. It is one thing to accept legitimate spheres of influence. It is another entirely to allow these to hold sway over freely chosen wishes of democratic, sovereign peoples. That represents not only a betrayal of the first order but bad policy as well. If NATO pursues a renewal agenda based on enhanced capabilities for deterrence, containment and balancing, it will be in a much stronger position to defend the values it has shared for sixty-seven years against the rapacious predations of a renegade state. Selective cooperation on issues such as counterterrorism and nonproliferation within a broader framework of competition offers the optimal route to making the new cool war with Russia as brief and painless as feasible. Moreover, if Washington can annually engage China in a strategic and economic dialogue at the highest levels, at a minimum it can do so with Europe as well. The course of the European project may be uncertain but both parties would benefit from more closely integrated and regular consultation on matters of shared interest and principle.

The Middle East

In the Middle East, a multiplicity of problems have arisen from a combination of Obama's retreat and mismanagement. His attempt to disentangle the United States from the region generated more problems than it solved. But there is little point rehearsing what might have been. We are where we are. Moreover, tempting as it is to leave the region to stew in its own juices, a strategy of extrication and balancing is only likely to require yet another new engagement. As Kenneth Pollack and Ray Takeyh remind us, "Washington ought to have learned from its long and painful history with the Middle East that ignoring the region's problems will not make them go away. Inevitably, they return, worse than before. And just as inevitably, handling those problems later requires far more time and energy – and blood and treasure – than solving them sooner does.[14] Moreover, chaos in the Arab world has offered the Kremlin a convenient opportunity to project power and mollify public opinion at home on such issues as the legitimacy of Putin's Mafia regime, confrontation with the West and Ukraine. Russians nostalgic for "imperial" glory revel in the neuralgic support for Damascus, close relations with Tehran and rapprochement with Egypt that pose as the restoration of the Kremlin's lost influence. With naval and land bases secured in the eastern Mediterranean, a warm-water Black Sea port restored in Crimea, and cruise missiles launched from the Caspian Sea to hit Syrian rebels 900 miles away, Russian military reach appears more impressive than at any time since the Cold War.

Thanks to Obama's ill-judged diplomacy, the United States now faces a choice of exclusively bad options: does it take sides in the growing cold and sectarian regional war or seek instead to play the rival forces off against each other, distancing itself from the Faustian pact with Riyadh that has long bedeviled the coherence of Washington's role? Or, as Robert Baer succinctly asked, "As an ally, would Iran be more reliable and more reasonable than the Sunnis, the sect we've so long placed such blind trust in?[15] Did the United States take the nuclear issue off the table in order to clear the decks for a tougher regional strategy to counter Iran's rush for regional hegemony? Or is the nuclear deal just the first act in a longer drama of retreat, retrenchment and accommodation that hands the keys of the Persian Gulf to its new Shia friends? The truth is hardly hiding in plain sight. But, as elsewhere, Washington remains master of its own fate to a greater extent than any other power. As Henry Kissinger notes, "The US must decide for itself the role it will play in the 21st century; the Middle East will be our most immediate – and perhaps most severe – test. At question is not the strength of American arms but rather American resolve in understanding and mastering a new world."[16]

In the short term, there exists little option after Obama but to hedge. The region from Morocco to Afghanistan is mired in a multidecade crisis that promises to worsen considerably before it recovers. Collateral damage and knock-on effects will continue before anything improves. The United States can do little to address the weakness of governing institutions in many Arab states that has aggravated the new complex of conflict. The guiding principle of Washington's response should be twofold: first, to preserve its own regional position from encroachment by outside great powers, most notably Russia and China; and second, to prefer order over chaos, and thereby support states that provide effective governance, even when that does not achieve preferred levels of democracy and human rights. As we have seen, there are worse things than cooperative but authoritarian states, not least when collective convulsion threatens to eviscerate the notion of nation-states altogether.

How those imperatives play out will partly depend on the path that key nations follow. Obama has left a stronger Iran shoring up a Syrian regime whose slaughter is a principal recruiting tool for ISIS. In the short to medium term, the imperatives of destroying ISIS, ensuring an orderly post-Assad transition and rolling back Iranian influence can only compel tactical adjustments that respond to the fluidity of the key regional actors. If Iran responds as enthusiasts for US rapprochement hope, and adopts a less destabilizing approach, then the notion of balancing competing players would not be so implausible. But it is highly doubtful that Tehran will retreat within its own borders to a Westphalian state role. Rather, Tehran will use the financial bonanza of the end of economic sanctions to reassert its own hegemonic ambitions. Particularly if Washington uses the JCPOA as an excuse to further disengage, it is highly likely that Iran's goals will become even more expansive and its policies more aggressive, believing that the United States no longer has the will or the capability to stop it. But the Iranian calculus can be affected and altered. If the United States redoubles its engagement in the region and acts decisively by providing real, meaningful assurances to its Gulf allies that it is genuinely concerned with protecting their security interests and pushing back hard on Tehran in other areas, particularly Syria, then the Iranians may well respond as they typically have previously when America has seriously flexed its muscles: by backing down.

Implementing the JCPOA with extreme vigilance is also of paramount importance if the United States is not to be obliged to shift from preventing to managing proliferation. The prudent course is to anticipate violations, expect them to go undetected or unconfirmed for lengthy periods and see Iran moving further toward operational nuclear weapons than the deal contemplates. Moreover, under paragraph 36 of the agreement, Iran can abandon its obligations any time it complains that other signatories have abandoned theirs. It is not difficult to imagine how such complaints could arise. The most useful short-term step to increase the deterrence capacity of the US, Israel and Arab allies would be for the next president to publicly commit the United States to a policy of deterrence, approve further defensive arms agreements and ask Congress to pass an authorization for use of military force (AUMF) in case Iran cheats.[17] That deterrent option would be strengthened further by increased naval and air deployments in the Gulf, prepositioning in the Middle East the US Air Force's Massive Ordnance Penetrator bombs – the 30,000 pound, precision-guided, "bunker-buster" weapons – that could penetrate any Iranian weapons production efforts hidden within mountain complexes. Leasing these to Israel would be another option. While proposals for more formal alliance arrangements, NATO-style, are totally implausible, and intra-Arab attempts at military cooperation have proven reliably stillborn, a US forward presence can lend some assurance to the many capitals disturbed by Tehran's ambitions. Moreover, given the glaring loopholes and inadequacy of inspection arrangements, it is difficult to envisage the forty-fifth president not having to once more endure another 2002–03 Iraq-style crisis over Iran's nuclear program and to contemplate whether or not airstrikes are necessary. The United States and its allies need to be well prepared for that contingency.

Obama's nuclear diplomacy only postponed, rather than cancelled, that day of reckoning and the months and years of diplomatic wrangling that may once more precede it.

Another consequence of that diplomacy is that any serious effort to end Syria's war will require the United States to choose between challenging Iran's Syrian land bridge to Hezbollah through more vigorous support for anti-Assad forces, or accepting a settlement that tacitly sanctions a Russian client state and a continued Iranian proxy army expanding on Israel's border. Sanctions relief amounts to roughly a quarter of Iran's annual GDP, which was approximately $415 billion in 2014. In historical terms, it also matches America's entire post-World War II plan for the reconstruction of Europe. If and when the Syrian civil war abates, most plausibly in some kind of federal arrangement, Israel may discover it is bordered to the north by either an Iranian-backed Alawite (sub)state, a Sunni Islamist state tied to Turkey or Saudi Arabia, or some other hostile entity. Thanks to Obama's incoherent improvisations, and despite back-channel attempts at anti-Iranian compacts with Sunni forces, Israel's geopolitical circumstances have become significantly more perilous. A dangerous neighborhood has deteriorated even further. The next US administration will likely confront another Israeli war in which the United States has no choice but to intervene, politically and perhaps militarily, to preserve the national security of the Jewish homeland.

Finally, but of most importance, the threat from ISIS will remain in need of direct US attention. ISIS numbers far exceed those that went to Afghanistan during the 1980s and 1990s, creating the same conditions that led to 9/11 but on a far greater magnitude. The Pentagon has struggled since 2014 to execute its mission of degrading and defeating ISIS, a reflection of the reality that "leading from behind" is easier to frame as a political slogan than an effective military operation. US civilian leaders need to encourage the Pentagon to do better but at the same time, military leaders need to think more creatively about how to speed up the fight. Absent the deployment of ground forces in large numbers, more targeted assistance and innovation in niche areas is likely to be needed, probably requiring a greater role for special operations personnel. With only around 3,000 US forces in Iraq, mostly "within the wire" on secure bases, the military cannot simply repeat strategies from 2007, when it had 185,000 troops spread across every area in the country. The Defense Department's $1.6 billion Iraq Train and Equip Fund, a scaled-down version of the massive programs that created Iraqi duplicates of US brigades in 2005–08, underperformed, training only 9,000 of 24,000 troops that were supposed to be fully trained and equipped by June 2015. At the same time, the world's most powerful air force was hamstrung in Iraq by a combination of strict rules of engagement and too few trusted on-the-ground spotters for airstrikes. At a minimum, both need to change, embedding some soldiers with Iraqi and other Arab boots on the ground and providing arms to the Kurdish *Peshmerga*, Sunni tribes and Syrian opposition. Over the longer term, only political changes are likely to reestablish some form of stability in either Syria or Iraq, but Iraq has permanently splintered into Sunni, Kurdish and Shia enclaves, and neither Iran nor Russia is likely to abandon its newfound influence to secure these. Only military defeat will end the allure of ISIS and only a well-equipped land army acting in concert with air power will prevail against the barbarians.

Reenergizing security by freer trade and securitizing energy
Building strong trade ties represents the most underrated but effective form of US global involvement. Allies desire it and adversaries fear it. Strengthening the global free trade regime represents seriously "smart power" as a trump card to play in the complex game of global influence. Moreover, with 25 percent of its GDP dependent on trade, the integration of the US economy into the world one represents an unescapable cornerstone of effective statecraft.

Renewing that aspect of strategy should form a key part of a post-Obama foreign policy. Remarkable progress has occurred since World War II on global trade that has increased prosperity around the world and lifted millions out of poverty. But the popular and political support that sustained this project has never been solid in the United States. Protectionists, focused on the most narrow, parochial and short-term interests, seek to defend a small segment of the American economy at the cost of the global economy and US global influence. Support for free trade faltered again after the financial crisis of 2008. The failure of the Doha round of trade talks, which remains open but stalled (having begun in 2001), appears to have marked the end of trade deals at the global level. Beginning with the 1947 General Agreement on Tariffs and Trade, their primary achievement has been to drive down the cost of tariffs on goods. Tariffs still exist, such as the EU's 10 percent tariff on car imports. The imperative now though is for the reform of the less visible barriers to services, which make up an ever growing part of economies.

The Obama administration eventually completed the passage through Congress of three trade agreements – with Panama, Colombia and South Korea – negotiated and signed by the Bush administration. In 2015, the African Growth and Opportunity Act was also renewed (a Bill Clinton-era law allowing Africans to sell many goods tariff-free to the United States). Echoing Clinton's experience with NAFTA, Obama also gained "fast-track" negotiating authority – Trade Promotion Authority – from Congress in June 2015, thanks to the support of most Republicans over the opposition of most Democrats. The latter should strongly assist, though it does not assure, passage of two comprehensive new agreements: TTIP and TPP. While recognizing the limits of trade to internal political transformations – increased commerce and prosperity has done little to alter the authoritarian political systems of Russia or China or transform their swords into ploughshares – both the economic benefits and the support offered to an open, economically liberal trading system by TTIP and TPP are potentially substantial.

Three additional steps would be especially useful.

First, regional projects need urgently to be ratified and expanded. Bilateral, regional and mega-regional free trade agreements offer the most realistic opportunity for progress. The geostrategic implications of success in the latter, especially, are potentially immense. At a time when Russia is actively promoting its Eurasian Economic Union of authoritarian countries and is not shy about engaging in dubious deal-making within Europe, Washington and Brussels need to make it easier for the countries of the Atlantic community to deal commercially with each other and to tighten business practices. TPP would also validate rebalancing to Asia. Together, they would consolidate the US position as lynchpin of the world's two largest trading blocs.

TTIP could be the most ambitious free trade agreement in history. It has the potential to help revitalize a dormant Atlanticism and add as much as $150, $120 and $130 billion to the economies of the EU, United States and the rest of the world, respectively. If successfully concluded, TTIP would constitute the most ambitious free trade agreement in history. This is partly because of its sheer scale, the EU and United States together representing about 45 percent of global output. But it is also because of the attempt to tackle not just tariffs but also nontariff barriers and regulation. The core purpose of TTIP is to forge a system of transatlantic cooperation that might serve as a blueprint for trade more generally – to benefit 800 million consumers, almost one-third of global trade and set high-standard global trade rules fit for the twenty-first century. Joint regulation also gives third countries a strong incentive to adapt their standards. The price of failure to achieve ratification after several years of talks might be prohibitively high, and cause lasting damage to transatlantic relations.

If ratified by Congress, TPP, similarly, offers important geostrategic gains in Asia. A shrewd US strategy can both integrate and liberalize Asian partners' economies while shaping China's own options for isolation or integration in the wider market. The 2015 economic downturn and devaluations by Beijing were illustrative of an unbalanced Chinese economy in need of help, and left room for the United States to assert itself in the East Asian region. The United States can also encourage Chinese participation in the international monetary system, as the most direct way to smooth the imbalances that brought down the world financial system less than a decade previously. The Chinese authorities should allow markets to find their own level, much as they sought to do in the currency markets, where China successfully asked the IMF to include the yuan in the basket of currencies that make up the fund's unit of account, known as special drawing rights. China's central bank devaluation of August 2015 can be seen as a small step toward a more market-determined exchange rate rather than a salvo in a trade war with the West.

Second, the United States can restart global trade and investment talks, either by restarting World Trade Organization talks or beginning a process to consider eventually merging TTIP and TPP. Whether or not renewed and assertive internationalism should integrate China into the TPP and accord Beijing greater say in multilateral institutions (such as enhanced voting shares in the World Bank and IMF) needs careful consideration and should be contingent on the broader path of Chinese actions as a revanchist or responsible player. Nor should those states outside the TTIP and TPP agreements be neglected. India, Brazil, Turkey and others should be encouraged to make further trade liberalization within the WTO. Although the domestic politics of areas such as reform of agricultural subsidies remains highly problematic, the benefits – material and strategic – are potentially substantial. Obama did not extend the AGOA to farm products, for instance, a move that could significantly improve African growth.

Third, the revitalization of the Atlantic and Pacific dimensions offered by trade can and should be complemented by efforts to harness the benefits of America's energy renaissance. One of the few clear-cut advances for national security since the 2000s has been the US energy revolution. Although fossil fuel power plants supply the United States with about 70 percent of its electricity, the shale gas industry has more than halved energy costs and played a key role in economic recovery (despite billions of dollars of subsidies, wind and solar power manage to supply only 5 percent of the nation's electricity). Where US influence generally was waning under Obama, the shale oil and gas markets provided an invaluable power surge.

America's displacement of Saudi Arabia as the world's biggest oil producer represents an advance of huge geopolitical importance. In 2014, the Organization of the Petroleum Exporting Countries (OPEC), led by Riyadh, initiated an economic oil war against the United States when it refused to cut production in November of 2014, as it typically does when oil prices drop. This was an attempt to drive some US shale oil producers bankrupt and stem the flow of North American shale oil onto the global market. OPEC increased oil production, which drove oil prices down to nearly $50, the price at which many shale producers fail to break even. But instead of halting shale oil production, the move begot a rapid consolidation and merging of companies that increased efficiencies and lowered production costs so that the marginal cost of shale oil can go lower and lower and still allow shale oil to compete on the global market. In short, the US shale oil industry was made leaner and meaner.

Spare capacity is now less than 2 million barrels per day compared to the 1980s oil glut when it exceeded 15 million bpd. This means that small changes in supply or demand can cause large changes in the oil price. This leads to significant price volatility, which should only increase in the coming years. While Saudi Arabia produces 10 million bpd, more than any other country, it has little-to-no extra capacity to adjust to sudden increases in demand, similar to other OPEC suppliers. OPEC can no longer control the price and supply as effectively as previously because there is too much outside supply and too much growing volatility in demand. A primary reason for the accelerated price decline is that Saudi Arabia, the world's "swing supplier" – the one that can most easily increase or decrease production – decided to keep pumping. The

Saudis knew that it hurt them but hoped it would damage everyone else more, especially post-sanctions Iran. Thus far, it has not worked. US firms have used technology and smart business practices to stay afloat. The return of Iran's oil – which markets assume will happen, albeit slowly – is another factor driving down prices. So, too, is the increasing energy efficiency of cars and trucks. In consequence, major oil-producing countries globally are facing a fiscal reckoning such as they have not seen in decades.

For US national security, these low oil prices offer a salutary way to deprive unsavory regimes around the globe of easy money. But this would also be aided by a US administration more willing to embrace a proactive energy strategy (beyond, as in 2015, tapping the strategic reserve to help offset the costs of its budget agreement). For example, the Obama administration removed the final bureaucratic obstacle preventing Royal Dutch Shell from drilling for oil beneath the Arctic Ocean, clearing the way for the company to complete exploratory wells. But the approval, granted by the Bureau of Safety and Environmental Enforcement in August 2015, only came after Shell spent nearly eight years and more than $7 billion overcoming regulatory, political, legal and logistical challenges. Moreover, Hillary Clinton signaled a move to the left on environmental policy should she reach the White House with a climate plan that commits the United States to obtaining 33 percent of its electricity from renewable sources by 2027, which exceeds Obama's goal to generate 20 percent of America's electricity by 2030. (Renewable energy accounts for just 7 percent of the nation's current electric power supply.) Although measures to address climate change and encourage renewables are desirable, Washington should adopt an "all of the above" approach to its energy security.

This is not least the case since, from a production standpoint, the contemporary oil war pits conventional oil against unconventional oil. While over half of the proven oil reserves in the world are generally under the control of OPEC, there are many more unconventional reserves (such as oil shale, heavy oils and tar sands) outside the Middle East. The implications of this are not well understood, even now. Contrary to some accounts, it does not mean that America is, or will shortly become, energy independent. Even with the ability to provide for its own energy needs from domestic supply alongside key hemispheric suppliers (Canada, Mexico, Venezuela and Brazil), this is not enough. Nor does it imply that – notwithstanding security issues – Washington need no longer concern itself about the Middle East. Oil is a fungible commodity. In the global economy, American jobs depend on international trade with partners who rely far more heavily than the United States on oil from the Middle East. Disruption to the flow of oil from the Gulf will sharply increase the global price of oil and affect not only US gasoline prices but also allies and global trade.

But if the energy revolution is not a panacea, it nonetheless offers potentially powerful benefits to the United States and the wider West. At minimum it offers a fallback position for the United States. But a creative policy would utilize the US global naval dominance to exploit its strong energy position as a powerful carrot. Lifting the ban on exports and the approval of natural gas sales would be the most obvious start, in order to reinforce established alliances. But in addition to formal allies, countries such as India should also be prioritized by Washington as recipients of US energy. Emerging powers across the world require reliable supply and such a contribution by the United States can positively add to the security of global energy flows. And although complete exclusion of Moscow from the European supply mix is not feasible, the United States should act in concert with the EU to deprive Russia of political leverage in key energy markets. The greater the economic ties, and the less the energy exposure, the more effective collaborative efforts to stabilizing world order and restraining both the incentives and capacity of revisionist states to upend the liberal international system will prove.

Reviving muscular internationalism

According to Officer Jim Malone in *The Untouchables*, the optimal way to approach gangsters is famously simple: "They pull a knife, you pull a gun. He sends one of yours to the hospital, you send one of his to the morgue. That's the Chicago way." But that particular teachable moment from his prepresidential hometown was apparently lost on Obama. Or, more accurately, the Windy City lesson applied only to Beltway politics; international affairs were altogether different.

As previous chapters noted, a central problem of the Obama era was the consistent absence of a credible coercive element to American diplomacy. As such, it was hardly surprising that Russia, China and Iran should press ahead when they encountered no significant resistance from the United States beyond less than warm words. Where Obama saw gestures of peaceful intent, others saw only a sheep in sheep's clothing. In a peculiar condition of strategic Stockholm Syndrome, Washington appeared beholden to its adversaries. For fear of provocation, America risked peace. But neither America's allies nor adversaries should again be left in any doubt as to whether the United States has "redlines" in foreign affairs, lest the underpinnings of global security are shattered. For all the drone strikes and targeted killings, Obama's was ultimately a 9/10 approach to a post-9/11 world. The administration itself implicitly conceded as much with the NMS of 2015, which testified to the array of strategic surprises that confronted the Obama administration during its second term. Moreover, the new strategy's emphasis on global disorder and rising threats – a stark contrast to the NMS of 2011 – offered a potent reminder that the president and Congress erred gravely when they imposed the trillion dollars of cuts on the US military. With an overarching platform of retrenchment, threats of force were too infrequently part of the diplomatic arsenal. When nominally there – as on Iran – Washington simply lacked, or lost, the credibility for them to be effective.

That lacuna needs to be addressed. Let us be clear, though, that muscular internationalism is not a euphemism for an itchy trigger finger. It is instead a commitment not to approach an adversary with an empty holster. Bellicosity is no more a synonym for leadership than diplomacy. In diplomatic terms, there was, and remains, a vast array of alternatives between unconditional negotiations and war. But that scale of escalation needs adversaries to be persuaded that all options genuinely are "on the table." And that, in turn, requires on occasion the actual threat, or employment, of force to deal with a specific case where merited. Moreover, sometimes unilateral US action will be necessary, not least when no viable multilateral options exist. But unlike the Obama administration, unilateral concessions – such as toward Iran, Russia and Cuba – should invariably be eschewed.

The use of coercive diplomacy applies to both the national interest and cases less directly implicating US security. Like so many UN resolutions, the "Responsibility to Protect" was proclaimed with solemn pledges after years of study and debate and, like so many UN resolutions, it has gone unobserved and unenforced. Even before ISIS came to prominence, Syria required safe havens protected by no-fly zones and limited airstrikes to stop the civilian population being bombed into submission and exodus by Assad. Failure to do so condemned millions to death and displacement, destabilized fragile neighboring states and created the biggest crisis Europe has faced since World War II. Failure to respond to Assad's use of chemical weapons – the most significant violation of the norm against their use since the Iran-Iraq War – was bad enough. The humanitarian tragedy was worse. The revelation by US intelligence agencies that efforts to force Syria to give up its chemical arsenal – hailed as a major foreign policy victory – actually failed, thanks to a "chain of misrepresentations" by the Assad regime, was the ultimate humiliation. Their possible use by ISIS against the Kurds in August 2015 was the tragically perverse result. From turning a blind eye to religious cleansing in the Middle East to tolerance of female genital mutilation in Africa, the last thing the UN has proven capable of is offering protection and security to those most in need. As Obama plaintively noted in 2013, the Security Council "demonstrated no inclination to act at all."

But why was that? Did the international community's latest iteration of failing to deliver on its pledge of "never again" in regard to ethnic cleansing and genocide have nothing to do with flawed US decision making? Or was the president psychologically projecting on a global scale what the former special advisor for transition in Syria termed the Obama administration's "pantomime of outrage"?[18] The next administration can at least confirm that Syria, Iraq, Ukraine, Iran and more besides represented episodic failures of US policy, not indelible features of a new international order.

America remains indispensable. There is no possibility of effective collective action in the absence of US participation or where the United States is indecisive or only partially committed. Certainly, America can no more compel others to follow its lead now than during the Cold War or "unipolar" era thereafter. There was no such golden age. But, as then, America can choose whether or not to lead, whether or not to make a difference. "It's not the job of the president of the United States to solve every problem in the Middle East," Obama declared in a June 15, 2015, news conference. True enough. But Syria represented not "every" problem but a very specific and unique humanitarian and strategic failure of the first order.

Economic sanctions offer another option to complement limited and specific US military intervention, one much favored by the Obama administration. But these are at best imperfect instruments. From the outset of the Ukraine crisis, the West acted on the premise that sanctions would induce Russia to modify its actions (an approach congenial to the United States, with only 1 percent of its GDP coming from trade with Russia). But while comprehensive sanctions that impose costs on mass publics are now out of favor, selective sanctions, though they can constrain capacity, do not constrain behavior. Their immediate impact is bearable. Only more severe measures can make a serious impact. For example, for all their vitriolic anti-Westernism, the Putin cabal does not look to their fellow BRICS for their families' schools, universities, holidays, medical treatment and investments, but to the United States and EU. Freezing Russian laundered money, prosecuting the Kremlin's accomplices, and denying visas to the Russian elite and their families represents a modest start. Denying Russia access to Western sources of credit and excluding Russia from the SWIFT bank transfer system offer additional coercive options, as do wider sanctions on key economic sectors such as oil, mining and defense. But even these measures ultimately do nothing to diminish Russia's most usable and effective form of power: military force.

Providing critical military assistance to allied forces and local auxiliaries is a crucial element in coercive diplomacy. In the case of Russia, providing such assistance to Ukraine would have devalued Moscow's advantage in negotiations. The Russian offensive of August 2014 won diplomatic concessions in Minsk that would not otherwise have been secured. The more devastating military offensive of January–February 2015, blatantly violating the first Minsk accord, produced a second agreement even more flawed – and once more breached – than the first. According to the second Minsk agreement, future elections, constitutional reform and border controls are contingent on the agreement of the separatists. As bridgeheads for Moscow's wider goals – "federalizing" Ukraine to ensure its loss of sovereignty or "non-bloc status" to enforce neutrality and thereby abandon a Western tilt – Russia's military card has been the key arbiter of diplomacy. Devaluing that by strengthening Kiev's military muscle was, and remains, vital. Would this be provocative to Moscow? Surely. But no more than placing Cruise and Pershing missiles in Western Europe was in the 1980s. Washington's adversaries invariably view US actions through a lens of provocation rather than assurance. That should not deter America from prudent steps that form part of a logically coherent approach.

Much the same could be said of the incoherent US approach to ISIS. ISIS is a genocidal and violent symptom of primarily political problems that have destabilized Iraq since 2003 and Syria since 2011. It is a truism that unless and until these political problems are successfully addressed, ISIS cannot be fully defeated. But even if one accepted the rationale for a minimalist approach, the United States had a reliable and courageous ally in the Kurdish regional government. The Pentagon could and should have directly armed Kurdish fighters, who were holding the line against ISIS in Iraq's north. Instead, the Obama administration stubbornly persisted in routing supplies through the government in Baghdad, lest it antagonize Baghdad and Ankara (fearful of an incipient Kurdish state on its borders). With the Iraq government a satrapy of Iran, Ankara as deeply unreliable a NATO ally as Pakistan is a non-NATO "frenemy" in South Asia, Iraqi forces making "Dad's Army" resemble the 82nd Airborne, and ISIS advancing across territory larger than the state of Indiana, this timidity made little strategic sense.

Much the same could also be said of the $500 million "train and equip" plan for Syria, approved by Congress in 2014, under which an overt program – run by US Special Operations forces and separate from a parallel covert program run by the CIA – was designed to generate more than 5,000 trained fighters a year who could help eliminate ISIS from Syria and then hold the ground. By helping to secure a safe zone in northern Syria, the force could facilitate humanitarian assistance and help provide greater security for the devastated population, in addition to pushing back the extremists. But the idea never had strong support from a White House allergic to Syrian intervention, and the mere fifty-four "graduates," trained at an expense of almost $42 million, were either killed, captured or ran away within weeks of their deployment in the field in the summer of 2015. The Division 30 debacle made the Bay of Pigs resemble the Normandy landings. But at least Kennedy inherited the former. The Syrian fiasco was entirely Obama's own making.

Minimalist tactics premised on training, outsourcing and incremental escalation cannot suffice. Politically, over the short term, that may appeal. But that is not a reliable recipe to secure a reversal of strategic fortunes. A complete overhaul of counterterrorism training and resourcing of foreign governments is necessary, along with new approaches to undermining the logistical infrastructure of terrorism, especially in financing. But the inconvenient yet unavoidable truth is that the United States will once again need to deploy ground forces in combat. Hopefully, that may not have to be against great power competitors, Russia and China, or rogue state adversaries such as Iran and North Korea. But almost certainly, it will involve Islamist jihadist forces waging transnational war. The only real questions are when, in what numbers and whether that deployment occurs in time and scope to be effective. There is a cyclical problem here, inasmuch as the United States needs to be placed once again on a war footing, without which the necessary unity of the political class and public will be wanting. But the political class needs to take the lead in articulating the realities of the threat matrix facing the United States and its allies, without which the public will – entirely reasonably – legitimately question the need for new commitments of blood and treasure.

A similar logic applies to cyber threats. Unfortunately, many accounts of cyber-attacks are discounted. Russia was responsible for penetrating the unclassified e-mail system used by the Joint Chiefs of Staff; a major Hollywood studio discovered its computers ruined; a sensitive US government trove of personnel information was stolen; corporate secrets were hacked and used for insider trading; major retailers and a healthcare provider were looted of customer data – yet the United States has been complacent and late in responding. Asymmetrical, and favoring a smaller, stealthy attacker over the defender, cyber-conflict does not fit neatly into other types of war, espionage and crime. Moreover, the concept of deterrence from the nuclear age – the idea of two cocked pistols preventing either side from shooting – offers limited comfort in a conflict in which attackers often can avoid identification until long after an attack. US cyber-weapons are also still largely secret and embedded in the intelligence community, precluding open debate, while the possibility of retaliation could cause even more harm to vulnerable US networks. But Washington needs to give cyber-attackers real pause and a credible threat of retaliation, one that can be seen in public as well as felt in private – whether through economic sanctions or a retaliatory assault in cyberspace.

The logic of forging a strong defense, maintaining a worldwide system of alliances, safeguarding a forward presence in every region, and drawing clear redlines that are unambiguously enforced is precisely in order to deter, but simultaneously be prepared for, war. Moreover, the unique position that Washington has occupied since 1991 has allowed it to intervene to bring pressure on other combatants to cease – or not escalate – their conflict, whether in the case of India and Pakistan in 2002 or Israel and Hezbollah in 2006. A reduced US presence, a less robust set of alliances and a more enfeebled military presence will retard that capacity. It is in the interests of neither the United States nor of a more peaceful and stable order. What repeatedly provoked and encouraged adversaries such as Putin and Khamenei was not strength but weakness and bluff.

Resuming strategic resolution

Leadership is ultimately about choosing: between rivalry and restraint, excessive and insufficient activism, risk and reward. Neat and clear moral choices are rarely on offer. Occasional failures, reversals and blowback are the price of an active international role. The struggle against the forces of militarism, Nazism and fascism occupied years. The Cold War endured for decades. But America and the West ultimately prevailed in what at times resembled the definition of a Sisyphean task. Successive administrations renewed containment and committed men and material to an existential struggle. Under constant threat of nuclear extinction, normal life went on apace. And underlying the diplomatic, economic and military dimensions was an ideological base that – despite assault from within and without – remained resolute in the belief in the superiority of the political, economic and social forms of organization adopted by the West.

That tradition merits reclamation. It offers an instructive path between both the strategic complacency, negligence and myopia of the Obama administration and the sterile confrontation and populist hysteria that sometimes accompanies Americanism "with its sleeves rolled up." In the face of nationalist and nihilistic threats, state and nonstate enemies, leadership must not only passively reflect narrow material demands but calmly and actively shape public opinion in a responsible direction. In a jungle inhabited by profoundly illiberal forces on the march, liberal democracy needs teeth, not squeamishness. During the Cold War, Americans did not allow the physical barriers offered by two large oceans to create mental barriers as to their vulnerability to foreign threats. But when JFK was shown evidence of Soviet ships heading for Cuba in October 1962, there was no chance that they were actually Chinese. Today, a Digital Pearl Harbor could occur but the identity of the attackers remain unknown or authorities be deliberately deceived. However tempting the promise of a peaceful retreat from the world may seem today, not retreating to Fortress America remains wise and prudent. Rather than being caught between the Scylla of domestic isolationism and the Charybdis of external eclipse, the political class can act in ways that both preclude the coalescing of disunited antagonists abroad and shore up public support at home, to extend and deepen American primacy for a long twilight struggle of generational duration.

In three senses, resolution may well be regarded as a conservative approach.

First, it seeks to conserve the existing liberal international order and patch up its fraying aspects. Much as the Cold War was waged on multiple fronts, so too must the struggles against authoritarian states and Islamist jihadism. Like the Cold War's end, where America was willing to strike a modus vivendi with the Soviet Union once its expansionist impulse was exhausted, so the United States can in principle live with "Islamism in one country." The problem remains, of course, that, like communism, Islamist ambitions – especially in their Salafist and Deobandi forms and in Iran – are unlikely to be satiated until the futility of their quest is made irrefutably clear. Islamist goals are less to join the family of nations than to become a single nation. Former army chief General Ray Odierno predicted in July 2015 that the fight against ISIS could take ten–twenty years, far longer than the three–five years usually offered by US military officials. The struggle against the broader cancer of Islamism may take still longer. Any other notion is being economical with the truth. For ISIS and its admirers, expansion is integral to the appeal of transnational Islamism and the combination of ideology, identity, grievance and mobilization that turns radicals to violence is supremely tough even to monitor, never mind prevent. In terms of intelligence collection, if tracking communists in the 1950s was akin to searching for a needle in a haystack, tracing Islamists resembles looking for a specific piece of hay in a haystack. The challenge for the rest of humanity is not likely to be short-lived.

Second, strategic resolution is an approach broadly favored by conservative internationalists, realists and hawks, for whom talking clearly and confidently about national security ought to be a first rather than a second language. But notwithstanding that ideological aspect, the left should also be able to support a New American Internationalism. From Russia and China to Iran and ISIS, the forces arrayed against the West are profoundly hostile to most causes that progressives hold dear, from gender equality and gay rights to freedom of (and from) religion. Perhaps now that the severity of the enemies of the open society is plain – though it could hardly have been more so than on 9/11 – the tactical exigencies of "resistance" to American "imperialism" can safely be abandoned. Unless, that is, progressives are no longer capable of moral indignation over mass slaughter of innocent civilians, groups such as ISIS that use rape and sex slavery as a recruiting tool, or the evisceration of entire nation-states? Not every problem can or should meet a military solution, but action to forestall fascists and prevent genocide can in the right circumstances prove both practical and noble. Kosovo proved that. Srebrenica, Rwanda, Darfur, the Congo and Syria showed the tragic scale of what happens when we turn our backs.

Third, while doubting the chances of its happening, resolution commends a return to greater constitutional balance and a less centralized national security decision-making process. The Romans knew the dangers of hubris. When they gave their victorious generals their Triumphs – gaudy marches into Rome to celebrate their success – the general would be reminded, "Remember, you are mortal." The most powerful officeholder in the world needs genuine advice, not sycophancy, and strategic as well as political counsel. A sound reorganization of national security making would eschew the politicized overcentralization and micromanagement of the Obama administration. The federal government has sufficient personnel to master the complexities of specific regions and nations while keeping the president focused on major priorities. The NSC would benefit from rationalization from its current bloated state of in excess of 400 staffers and the White House could usefully revisit the Bush 41 model of organization. A genuine team, not necessarily of rivals, but of independent and experienced foreign policy practitioners and thinkers would represent a better source of strategic planning and crisis management than reliance on a coterie of personally loyal political advisors.

Greater involvement of Congress, from notification to consultation, would also assist the construction of a genuinely national policy, however much contemporary partisanship militates against comity. Major arms control agreements with historic adversaries should be conducted through treaties, not pacts. Even in the case of the latter, formal approval votes would constitute a basic test for a representative democracy. Avoiding undisclosed side agreements in nuclear deals that, remarkably, neither the executive nor the Congress know the contents of, would also be a minimal step toward appropriately rebalancing executive-legislative relations. The next president should not rely on back-channels to reach out to his fellow foreign policy principals, fellow lawmakers and people, never mind foreign leaders.

Despite Obama's drafting America's letter of resignation from global leadership, the rest of the world has yet to accept it. Despite an Obama Doctrine so modest as to be meaningless, American power is not yet at a tipping point. Prudence dictates that the worst unforced error would be overestimating the risks posed by state and nonstate forces and, thereby, bring them into being through amplifying their importance or acting rashly to meet their challenge. The five wars fought by the United States since World War II all commenced with relative enthusiasm. But hawks did not prevail at their end, when public opinion shifted and they were left in a minority. The United States should not engage in international conflicts if, at the beginning, the end cannot be explained and if the public is unwilling to sustain the effort needed to achieve that end. But once committed, premature exits, as we saw in Iraq, are a recipe for instability, not tranquility. In Afghanistan, the right approach for the United States is not to pull out entirely by the end of 2016 – as the Obama administration intended – but to retain several bases and several thousand US and other NATO coalition troops for the foreseeable future. Moreover, while an American presence can be a source of intermittent tension from Japan to Iraq, its absence is typically more worrisome and conducive to instability.

That said, now is not the time for a complacent insularity. The multiple burdens facing Washington – to contain China's ascendancy, confront and deter Russian aggression, defeat and destroy ISIS, and retard Islamism – are generational challenges. Like the Cold War's challenge, this does not mean impeding daily life. Familiar homilies – "if we alter our ways of life, the terrorists will have won" – hardly stand up to serious scrutiny. Minor inconveniences at airports matter nothing in the broader context. Indeed, it is the conceit that they do that offers grist to charges about Western decadence. Oppressive national security is hardly deterring emigration to the West. History teaches us that violent ideologies outlive their adherents and that confronting the ideology – the real "root cause" of terror – should be as much a target as the murderous leaders and foot soldiers who are its ugly symptoms.

Nor does resolution imply a static mind-set. There is ample reason to adopt a "pay-as-you-go" approach. If rivals genuinely alter their policies, there ought to be reward. But if gambits such as the Ukraine war or South China Sea provocations are made, they should meet a firm response within a reasonable time frame. Within any serious strategy, there is room for tactical adjustment and even reversals of policy when appropriate. Reagan, after all, braved conservative censure in reaching out to Gorbachev after the coldest of periods in the Cold War from 1981 to 1985. George W. Bush, much criticized for his stubbornness and blinkered views, incurred immense criticism for backing the surge in 2007. Should a truly democratic Iran emerge and abandon its hegemonic aspirations, a Chinese leadership accept rather than subvert existing norms or a responsible Russian president genuinely seek to join the community of nations, the United States should respond generously and rapidly. Resolution need not imply sticking to a policy no matter the evidence of its manifest failure. That represents more a description of Obama's ideologically driven approach than most of his predecessors.

The Chinese sage Lao Tzu, in his sixth-century BC classic text, the *Tao Te Ching*, advised that the wise man "never expects results; thus he is never disappointed." But risking disappointment is incumbent on leaders. No other great power holds the full spectrum combination of resources and capabilities possessed by the United States to shape history toward positive outcomes. Whatever the fashionable *nom de jour* – rising, resurgent, returning powers (as China, India, Iran and Russia view themselves) – the United States retains primacy and can choose its path forward with more autonomy than any other power. In their way, the Bush and Obama presidencies have offered a compelling synthesis for the years ahead; 9/11 showed the reality of the threat America faces and the limits to the type of transformational agenda adopted by Bush. The Obama years illustrated the dangers of disengagement, retrenchment and misreading adversaries' intentions. Post-Obama foreign policy thus needs recrafting to impress upon Americans at large the generational and multifront struggle that confronts the West – one that lacks the binary ideological dimension and bipolar structure of the Cold War but that nonetheless is predicated upon foes who seek the overturning of the liberal order of the past seventy years. But it must also recognize, as part of that generational struggle, the limits of US power to transform others. For years to come, given institutional inertia, political division and the absence of more compelling alternatives, the United States must exert its efforts through the layers of supranational institutions that make up the creaking global architecture of global order. In this sense, it makes little sense to frame global futures in terms of a G-zero, G-2 or G-20. All of these, and more besides, will coexist in different forms and on different issues simultaneously. But it remains the case that there is no other power within the overlapping contours of that intersecting architecture that can coordinate and shape outcomes better than a genuinely proactive and committed United States. Periodic disappointment is worth the attempt.

After Obama

"America, I'm pretty certain, is going to be the indispensable nation for the remainder of this century just like it was the last one," President Obama confidently declared in 2015.[19] If his successor can remedy Obama's failings, the forty-fourth president may well be proved correct.

Although cynics might regard Dean Acheson's characterization of the post-World War II UK as newly applicable to a United States that "has lost an empire but not yet found a role," reports of the end of the American Century are premature. Nonetheless, perhaps we are all weary realists now, anesthetized into fatalism by Obama's risk aversion, legalism and studied silence in the face of genocidal tragedies, even where their adverse strategic implications aggravate the humanitarian outrage. The 2017 presidential inauguration is unlikely to reference paying any price (not enough dollars left), bearing any burden (not enough willpower) or ending tyranny (not enough willing converts or assured positive outcomes). No one expects, and few want, a new American sheriff to arrive in town and call up a posse to drive out the bad guys. Painful experience has proven that instant democracy is not possible. In those many nations where the conditions for democratization are absent, rebellions are apt to produce either anarchy or new illiberal and authoritarian regimes antipathetic to core American interests. Like all nations, the US struggles to balance principle and national interests, while complexity characterizes most conflicts and unintended consequences are the habitual accompaniment to intervention.

But unintended consequences attend inaction as well. The United States has a profound and enduring stake in world order. Leaving it to others has not worked out well previously and will not now. Despite an era of diminished ambitions, parochial obsessions with internal party politics and "celebrity" personalities, and a self-consciously frugal superpower, defeatism need not triumph. Because we cannot intervene everywhere does not mean we cannot, and should not, intervene anywhere. And intervention does not mean all-or-nothing. For a unique nation that is also a universal idea, insularity is especially problematic to the American DNA. American influence and international order have been thoroughly interwoven with a strong US forward presence for decades. The next president can move on resolutely from the aberrant Obama era and maintain that it is the policy of the United States to maintain American primacy, strengthen defense, broaden and deepen alliances, preserve an open global economy and prevail over revanchist forces opposing and undermining the West from without and within. It has, after all, been done before, under American auspices. And if the atypical Obama interlude is successfully transcended, then once more the world will have confirmation of Churchill's wisdom that, "You can always count on Americans to do the right thing – after they've tried everything else."

That is a comforting prospect, especially to those of us outside the United States who remain all too aware of the profound debt owed, and the national security that still relies disproportionately upon, a steadfast and internationalist Washington – and who adamantly do not wish America to go home. Regrettably, however, the next US administration will confront the consequences of Obama's foreign policy failures from a geopolitical and strategically weaker position. Short-term economies and domestic electoral gains have been traded for higher long-term strategic risks at greater potential long-run costs in American blood and treasure. All kinds of endemic problems, animosities and conflicts that have had little or nothing to do with Washington account for today's unstable world order. But, as one distinguished historian noted, "the abrogation by the world's leading power of its leadership responsibilities has contributed to the contemporary tragedy we are witnessing. Moreover – and more importantly – it is setting the stage for a future in which US leaders may be asked to take risks far greater than those Obama sidestepped in order to contain the cascading consequences of his inaction, inexperience, and his over-abundance of caution.'[20]

The past, as L. P. Hartley famously remarked, is a foreign country, "they do things differently there." There, America sought not to lead from behind nor downsize defense in the face of rising security threats. There, the United States was as eager to defeat as engage its adversaries. There, presidents concluded landmark negotiations without unseen "side agreements" and with bipartisan congressional support, or walked away from unsatisfactory accords, regard-less of the consequences for their personal "legacy." There, presidents were under no illusions as to the nature of the oppressive regimes with which they dealt or the reliability of parchment barriers to aggression. And there, peace through strength was the leitmotif of US global power and influence. That is a foreign country well worth revisiting. And in spite of Obama's best efforts at transformation, it is not yet too late to do so. Grand strategy needs to be respectfully mindful of, but not paralyzed by, limits – to aspire to more than international minimalism and the least that we can do. With will and determin-ation, the forty-fifth president can recalibrate the US approach and restore its traditional role as custodian of global order, something inimical to the enemies of liberty that numerous friends of the United States are eager to see. But it is exclusively up to Americans to choose whether or not to reverse the closing of the American strategic mind and bring to an end Obama's premortem on American power.

Notes

1. A return to strategy

1. www.whitehouse.gov/the-press-office/2012/01/24/remarks-president-state-union-address
2. The organization transliterates from Arabic as *al-Dawlah al-Islamiyah fi al-'Iraq wa al-Sham* abbreviated as Da'ish or DAESH, referred to in the West variously as the Islamic State of Iraq and the Levant (ISIL), the Islamic State of Iraq and Syria or the Islamic State of Iraq and al-Sham (ISIS), or Islamic State (IS). Herein, ISIS is the preferred usage.
3. http://foreignpolicy.com/2014/06/04/obamas-dont-do-stupid-shit-foreign-policy/
4. http://thebulletin.org/timeline
5. www.whitehouse.gov/the-press-office/remarks-president-barack-obama-prague-delivered
6. www.nytimes.com/2015/04/06/opinion/thomas-friedman-the-obama-doctrine-and-iran-interview.html?_r=0
7. www.whitehouse.gov/the-press-office/2015/09/28/remarks-president-obama-united-nations-general-assembly
8. *The Economist* April 11, 2015, p. 11.
9. Henry Kissinger, *World Order: Reflections on the Character of Nations and the Course of History* (London: Allen Lane, 2014).
10. www.whitehouse.gov/the-press-office/2013/08/31/statement-president-syria
11. www.wsj.com/articles/the-iran-deal-and-its-consequences-1428447582
12. www.whitehouse.gov/the-press-office/2015/09/28/remarks-president-obama-united-nations-general-assembly
13. www.whitehouse.gov/blog/2009/01/21/president-barack-obamas-inaugural-address

2. Strategic sabbatical: lessons of Obama's failure

1. Barack Obama, *The Audacity of Hope: Thoughts on Reclaiming the American Dream* (New York: Crown Publishers, 2006), pp. 302–3.

2. www.gallup.com/poll/1726/Presidential-Ratings-Issue-Approval.aspx
3. www.pewresearch.org/fact-tank/2014/09/04/5-takeaways-on-how-americans-view-a-world-in-crisis/
4. Jeffrey Goldberg, "Hillary Clinton: 'Failure' to Help Syrian Rebels Led to the Rise of ISIS," *The Atlantic* August 10, 2014, at: www.theatlantic.com/international/archive/2014/08/hillary-clinton-failure-to-help-syrian-rebels-led-to-the-rise-of-isis/375832/
5. Leon Panetta, *Worthy Fights: A Memoir of Leadership in War and Peace* (New York: Penguin Press, 2014).
6. www.foreignpolicy.com/articles/2014/09/09/national_insecurity_obama_foreign_policy
7. Vali Nasr, *The Dispensable Nation: American Foreign Policy in Retreat* (New York: Doubleday, 2013), p. 12.
8. See Colin Dueck, *The Obama Doctrine: American Grand Strategy Today* (New York: Oxford University Press, 2015).
9. www.nationalreview.com/article/419153/global-pottersville-victor-davis-hanson
10. For a dispassionate and compelling critique of "offshore balancing," see Hal Brands, "Fools Rush Out? The Flawed Logic of Offshore Balancing," *The Washington Quarterly* 38 (2) 2015, pp. 7–28.
11. www.foreignpolicy.com/articles/2014/09/09/national_insecurity_obama_foreign_policy
12. Robert Kagan, *The World America Made* (New York: Alfred Knopf, 2012), p. 86.
13. www.npr.org/2014/12/29/372485968/transcript-president-obamas-full-npr-interview
14. Eric Edelman and Ray Takeyh, "On Iran, Congress Should Just Say No," *Washington Post* July 17, 2015, at: www.washingtonpost.com/opinions/on-iran-congress-should-just-say-no/2015/07/17/56e366ae-2b30-11e5-bd33-395c05608059_story.html
15. Ray Takeyh, "The Payoff for Iran," *Washington Post* June 28, 2015, at: www.washingtonpost.com/opinions/the-payoff-for-iran/2015/06/28/6c8d58ac-1c26-11e5-bd7f-4611a60dd8e5_story.html?hpid=z7
16. Michael Mandelbaum, "Nuclear Arms Control, Then and Now," *The American Interest* April 22, 2015, at: www.the-american-interest.com/2015/04/22/nuclear-arms-control-then-and-now/
17. See Emma Sky, *The Unravelling: High Hopes and Missed Opportunities in Iraq* (London: Atlantic Books, 2015), chapters 19–20.
18. www.whitehouse.gov/the-press-office/2011/09/21/remarks-president-obama-address-united-nations-general-assembly
19. "The Post-American Middle East," *Foreign Affairs* 94 (6) 2015.
20. Michael O'Hanlon, "Obama's Military Policy: Down-Size While Threats Rise," *The Wall Street Journal* October 28, 2015, at: www.wsj.com/article_email/obamas-military-policy-down-size-while-threats-rise-1446073142-lMyQjAxMTE1MzIxOTIyOTk4Wj
21. www.foreignpolicyi.org/content/national-security-leaders-urge-congress-increase-defense-spending
22. Mark Urban, *The Edge: Is the Military Dominance of the West Coming to an End?* (London: Little, Brown, 2015), pp. 24–25.
23. Ibid. p. 118.

24. Remarks by the president, "A Foreign Policy for the Global Age," Address to the University of Nebraska at Kearney, Cushing Health and Sports Center, December 8, 2000, at: http://fas.org/news/usa/2000/usa-001208zws.htm.
25. Ian Bremmer, *Superpower: Three Choices for America's Role in the World* (London: Portfolio/Penguin, 2015), p. 164.
26. W. B. Yeats, *Collected Poems* (London: Picador, 1990), pp. 210–11.
27. David Hammond, "Mapped: How the World Became More Violent," at: www .telegraph.co.uk/news/worldnews/big-question-kcl/11711266/Mapped-How-the-world-became-more-violent.html
28. Quoted in Justin Webb, "Americans Warn Europe: You're on Your Own," *The Times* June 12, 2015, p. 24.
29. Henry M. Paulson, *Dealing with China: An Insider Unmasks the New Economic Superpower* (London: Headline, 2015), p. 402.

3. "45": prospects for renewal P. 47

1. www.vox.com/a/barack-obama-interview-vox-conversation/obama-foreign-policy-transcript
2. Adam J. Berinsky, *In Time of War: Understanding American Public Opinion from World War II to Iraq* (Chicago, IL: University of Chicago Press, 2009).
3. George Friedman and Meredith LeBard, *The Coming War with Japan* (New York: St. Martin's Press, 1991).
4. Zbigniewi Brzezinski, "From Hope to Audacity: Appraising Obama's Foreign Policy," *Foreign Affairs* 89 (1) 2010, pp. 28–30.
5. Jonathan Rynhold, *The Arab-Israeli Conflict in American Political Culture* (New York: Cambridge University Press, 2015).
6. http://i2.cdn.turner.com/cnn/2015/images/08/20/rel8c.-.iran.pdf
7. www.people-press.org/2015/09/08/support-for-iran-nuclear-agreement-falls/ #survey-report
8. Trade promotion authority means that the executive branch can conclude a trade agreement that Congress must then vote for or against, without the option of being able to pass amendments to the negotiated deal.
9. www.state.gov/s/l/treaty/pending/
10. www.whitehouse.gov/the-press-office/2015/08/05/remarks-president-iran-nuclear-deal
11. "President Obama Lashes Out at Iran Deal Critics," editorial, *Washington Post* August 11, 2015, at: www.washingtonpost.com/opinions/president-obamas-partisan-defense-of-the-iran-deal/2015/08/11/24f75c76-405d-11e5-9561-4b3dc93e3b9a _story.html?hpid=z3
12. Robert Kagan, *Paradise and Power: America and Europe in the New World Order* (London: Atlantic Books, 2003).
13. Benjamin I. Page and Marshall M. Bouton, *The Foreign Policy Disconnect: What Americans Want from Our Leaders But Don't Get* (Chicago, IL: University of Chicago Press, 2006).
14. Charles A. Kupchan and Peter L. Trubowitz, "The Illusion of Liberal Internationalism's Revival," *International Security* 35 (1) 2010, p. 96.

15. Miroslav Nincic and Monti Narayan Datta, "Of Paradise, Power, and Pachyderms," *Political Science Quarterly* 122 (2) 2007, p. 253.
16. Peter Hays Gries, *The Politics of American Foreign Policy: How Ideology Divides Liberals and Conservatives over Foreign Affairs* (Stanford, CA: Stanford University Press, 2014), p. 269.
17. "Beyond Red vs. Blue: The Political Typology," *Pew Research Center for the People and the Press* 2011, p. 89. www.people-press.org/files/legacy-pdf/Beyond-Red-vs-Blue-The-Political-Typology.pdf
18. "Public Sees U.S. Power Declining as Support for Global Engagement Slips," *Pew Research Center* December 3, 2013. www.people-press.org/2013/12/03/public-sees-u-s-power-declining-as-support-for-global-engagement-slips/
19. www.people-press.org/2013/12/03/public-sees-u-s-power-declining-as-support-for-global-engagement-slips/
20. Jeffrey Jones, "Americans Oppose U.S. Military Involvement in Syria," *Gallup* May 31, 2013. www.gallup.com/poll/162854/americans-oppose-military-involvement-syria.aspx
21. www.people-press.org/2013/12/03/public-sees-u-s-power-declining-as-support-for-global-engagement-slips/
22. Ibid.
23. Christopher Gelpi, Peter D. Feaver and Jason Reifler, *Paying the Human Costs of War: American Public Opinion and Casualties in Military Conflicts* (Princeton, NJ: Princeton University Press, 2009), p. 236.
24. www.realclearpolitics.com/epolls/other/direction_of_country-902.html
25. www.people-press.org/2015/02/26/democrats-have-more-positive-image-but-gop-runs-even-or-ahead-on-key-issues/
26. www.gallup.com/poll/183575/fewer-view-iraq-afghanistan-wars-mistakes.aspx
27. http://msnbcmedia.msn.com/i/MSNBC/Sections/A_Politics/6_22_PollPDF.pdf
28. http://edition.cnn.com/2015/06/03/politics/george-w-bush-favorability-ratings/
29. www.people-press.org/2015/07/22/a-year-later-u-s-campaign-against-isis-garners-support-raises-concerns/
30. Dina Smeltz, Ivo Daalder, Karl Friedhoff and Craig Kafura, *America Divided: Political Partisanship and US Foreign Policy* (Chicago: The Chicago Council on Global Affairs, 2015).
31. www.gallup.com/poll/184193/racism-edges-again-important-problem.aspx?utm_source=position5&utm_medium=related&utm_campaign=tiles
32. "The Most Interesting Man in American Politics: The Reinventions of Rand Paul" *Time* October 17, 2014.
33. Governor Chris Christie of New Jersey, e.g., titled his two-page foreign and national security policy briefing, "Re-establishing American Leadership" and subdivided this into three sections on "A Stronger National Defense," "Strong, Reliable Intelligence" and "Stand with Our Allies and Stand Up to Our Adversaries," at: https://d7oh9a36p82zs.cloudfront.net/Ccpres2016/base/assets/1-0-1/production/Chris-Christie-ForeignPolicy.pdf.
34. Marco Rubio, "Restoring America's Strength: My Vision for America," *Foreign Affairs* 94 (5) 2015, pp. 108–15.
35. https://jeb2016.com/full-remarks-taking-on-islamic-terrorism/?lang=en&wpisrc=nl_daily202&wpmm=1

36. Colin Dueck, *Hard-Line: The Republican Party and US Foreign Policy since WWII* (Princeton, NJ: Princeton University Press, 2010).
37. www.nytimes.com/imagepages/2008/09/01/us/politics/20080901_POLL_ GRAPHIC.html
38. Geoffrey Kabaservice, *Rule and Ruin: The Downfall of Moderation and the Destruction of the Republican Party, from Eisenhower to the Tea Party* (New York: Oxford University Press, 2012), p. 385.
39. www.schumer.senate.gov/newsroom/press-releases/my-position-on-the-iran-deal
40. Ed O'Keefe, "Jeb Bush: Obama and Clinton's Iraq Withdrawal 'Premature' and a 'Fatal Error'" *Washington Post* August 11, 2015, at: www.washingtonpost .com/news/post-politics/wp/2015/08/11/jeb-bush-obama-and-clintons-iraq-withdrawal-premature-and-a-fatal-error/?wpisrc=nl_daily202&wpmm=1
41. http://nationalinterest.org/feature/ghosts-obama-hillary-clintons-foreign-policy-problem-13568?page=3
42. Kurt M. Campbell and Michael E. O'Hanlon, *Hard Power: The New Politics of National Security* (New York: Basic Books, 2006).
43. E. J. Dionne, Jr, *Why The Right Went Wrong: Conservatism – From Goldwater to the Tea Party and Beyond* (New York: Simon and Schuster, 2016).

4. Reversing declinism: toward a second American century? *p. 72*

1. Robert S. Singh, *Barack Obama's Post-American Foreign Policy: The Limits of Engagement* (London: Bloomsbury, 2012).
2. Karen DeYoung, "Dozens of Retired Generals, Admirals Back Iran Deal," *Washington Post* August 11, 2015, at: www.washingtonpost.com/world/national-security/retired-generals-and-admirals-back-iran-nuclear-deal/2015/08/11/bd26f6ae-4045-11e5-bfe3-ff1d8549bfd2_story.html
3. Bruce Jones, *Still Ours to Lead: America, Rising Powers, and the Tension Between Rivalry and Restraint* (Washington, DC: Brookings Institution Press, 2014).
4. http://blogs.wsj.com/washwire/2015/01/22/americas-decline-era-ends-just-in-time-for-2016/
5. www.gallup.com/poll/181793/americans-split-worth-no-economically .aspx?utm_source=Economy&utm_medium=newsfeed&utm_campaign=tiles
6. *USA Today/Gallup* December 10–12, 2010.
7. Ibid.
8. Ibid.
9. Ibid.
10. The results are from a June 1–4, 2013 Gallup survey. An additional 10 percent say they are moderately proud to be an American, leaving 3 percent who say they are "only a little proud" and 1 percent who say they are "not at all proud."
11. June 1–4, 2013 *Gallup* survey.
12. Quoted in Nicholas Kristof, "U.S.A., Land of Limitations?" *The New York Times* Sunday Review August 8, 2015.
13. www.washingtonpost.com/blogs/govbeat/wp/2015/03/03/food-stamp-reliance-is-up-in-every-single-state-since-2000/?wpisrc=nl_pmpol&wpmm=1
14. www.cbo.gov/sites/default/files/114th-congress-2015-2016/reports/50 250-LongTermBudgetOutlook-3.pdf

15. Thomas E. Mann and Norman J. Ornstein, *It's Even Worse Than It Looks: How the American Constitutional System Collided with the New Politics of Extremism* (New York: Basic Books, 2012), p. xiv.
16. See James Piereson, *Shattered Consensus: The Rise and Decline of America's Postwar Political Order* (New York: Encounter Books, 2015), pp. 352–56.
17. www.washingtonpost.com/politics/poll-trump-carson-top-gop-race-clinton-leads-dems-but-support-drops/2015/09/13/7961a820-58c2-11e5-8bb1-b488d231bba2_story.html
18. Francis Fukuyama, "America in Decay: The Sources of Political Dysfunction," *Foreign Affairs* 93 (5) 2014, pp. 25–26.
19. Lloyd N. Cutler, "To Form a Government," *Foreign Affairs* 59 (1) 1980, p. 127.
20. Paul Kennedy, *The Rise and Fall of The Great Powers: Economic Change and Military Conflict 1500–2000* (London: Fontana, 1989).
21. www.digitalnpq.org/archive/2001_fall/colossus.html
22. John Darwin, *After Tamerlane: The Rise and Fall of Global Empires, 1400–2000* (New York: Penguin, 2008), p. 485.
23. Dominic Tierney, *The Right Way to Lose a War: America in an Age of Unwinnable Conflicts* (New York: Little, Brown and Company, 2015).
24. http://foreignpolicy.com/2015/08/13/campaign-consequences-us-presidential-election-gop-iran-trump-immigrants/?wp_login_redirect=0
25. Fareed Zakaria, *The Post-American World* (New York: Allen Lane, 2008), pp. 4–5.
26. Graham Allison, "The Thucydides Trap: Are the US and China Headed for War?" *The Atlantic* September 24, 2015, at: www.theatlantic.com/international/archive/2015/09/united-states-china-war-thucydides-trap/406756/
27. John Updike, *Toward the End of Time* (New York: Random House, 1997).
28. P. W. Singer and August Cole, *Ghost Fleet: A Novel of the Next World War* (New York: Houghton Mifflin Harcourt, 2015).
29. www.defense.gov/Portals/1/Documents/pubs/2015_China_Military_Power_Report.pdf
30. http://pages.uoregon.edu/kimball/Putin.htm
31. "Russia Gets Ready for 'War with West'," *The Times* August 12, 2015, p. 11. www.thetimes.co.uk/tto/news/uk/defence/article4524600.ece
32. Paul Lettow, "Have We Hit Peak America? The Sources of US Power and the Path to National Renaissance," *Foreign Policy* July/August, 2014, pp. 54–63, at: http://foreignpolicy.com/2014/07/03/have-we-hit-peak-america/; Joseph Nye, *Is the American Century Over?* (Cambridge, UK: Polity Press, 2015).
33. Stephen Brooks and William Wohlforth, *World Out of Balance: International Relations and the Challenge of American Primacy* (Princeton, NJ: Princeton University Press, 2008).
34. Niall Ferguson, *Colossus: The Rise and Fall of the American Empire* (London: Allen Lane, 2004), p. 3.
35. The "Soft Power 30" is a ranking of thirty countries around the world, based on a composite index that measures and compares the resources that determine a country's soft power. It contains sixty-six metrics across six categories: Government, Culture, Education, Global Engagement, Enterprise and Digital. The top ten for 2015, by ranking, were Britain, Germany, United States, France, Canada, Australia, Switzerland, Japan, Sweden and the Netherlands. http://softpower30.portland-communications.com/
36. www.youtube.com/watch?v=QnkHyG8u54E

5. The way forward: a new American internationalism ᴾ⁹⁸

1. Barry Posen, *Restraint: A New Foundation for US Grand Strategy* (Ithaca, NY: Cornell University Press, 2015).
2. Ian Bremmer, *Superpower: Three Choices for America's Role in the World* (New York: Portfolio/Penguin, 2015).
3. It is perhaps telling that Bremmer's publisher, Penguin, classified the book in "Economics" rather than "Politics."
4. Quoted in Peter Foster, "It's Farewell to a Nation of Two Tribes that Scarcely Meet," *Sunday Telegraph* August 9, 2015, p. 16.
5. Colin Dueck, *The Obama Doctrine: American Grand Strategy Today* (New York: Oxford University Press, 2015), p. 218.
6. It was found that 18.9 percent of lawmakers had either served, or were serving, in the military during the 114th Congress (2015–16). This is a decline from earlier decades when, for example, 64 percent of the 97th Congress (1981–82) and 73 percent of the 92nd Congress (1971–72) were veterans. See Jennifer E. Manning, *The 114th Congress: A Profile* (Washington, DC: CRS Report 7-5700, June 11, 2015), at: www.fas.org/sgp/crs/misc/R43869.pdf
7. www.nrdc.org/food/files/wasted-food-ip.pdf
8. Robert Gilpin, *War and Change in World Politics* (New York: Cambridge University Press, 1983), p. 194.
9. http://nationalinterest.org/feature/ghosts-obama-hillary-clintons-foreign-policy-problem-13568?page=3
10. Jeffrey Bader, *Obama and China's Rise* (Washington, DC: Brookings Institution Press, 2012), p. 149.
11. www.defense.gov/Portals/1/Documents/pubs/2011-National-Military-Strategy.pdf
12. www.jcs.mil/Portals/36/Documents/Publications/2015_National_Military_Strategy.pdf
13. Matthew Kroenig, "Facing Reality: Getting NATO Ready for a New Cold War," *Survival* 57 (1) 2015, p. 65.
14. Kenneth M. Pollack and Ray Takeyh, "Near Eastern Promises: Why Washington Should Focus on the Middle East," *Foreign Affairs* 93 (3) 2014, p. 105.
15. Robert Baer, *The Devil We Know: Dealing With the New Iranian Superpower* (New York: Three Rivers Press, 2008), p. 251.
16. Henry A. Kissinger, "A Path Out of the Middle East Collapse," *The Wall Street Journal* October 16, 2015, at: www.wsj.com/articles/a-path-out-of-the-middle-east-collapse-1445037513
17. Michael Mandelbaum, "How to Prevent an Iranian Bomb: The Case for Deterrence," *Foreign Affairs* 94 (6) 2015, pp. 19–24.
18. Frederic C. Hof, "America's Self-Inflicted Wound in Syria," *Foreign Policy* August 21, 2015, at: http://foreignpolicy.com/2015/08/21/americas-self-inflicted-wound-in-syria/
19. www.vox.com/a/barack-obama-interview-vox-conversation/obama-foreign-policy-transcript
20. David Rothkopf, "The Curse of the Obama Doctrine," *Foreign Policy* September 3, 2015, at: http://foreignpolicy.com/2015/09/03/the-curse-of-the-obama-doctrine-middle-east-arab-world/

Bibliography

Books

Bader, Jeffrey. *Obama and China's Rise* (Washington, DC: Brookings Institution Press, 2012).

Baer, Robert. *The Devil We Know: Dealing with the New Iranian Superpower* (New York: Three Rivers Press, 2008).

Berinsky, Adam J. *In Time of War: Understanding American Public Opinion from World War II to Iraq* (Chicago, IL: University of Chicago Press, 2009).

Bremmer, Ian. *Superpower: Three Choices for America's Role in the World* (New York: Portfolio/Penguin, 2015).

Brooks, Stephen and William Wohlforth. *World Out of Balance: International Relations and the Challenge of American Primacy* (Princeton, NJ: Princeton University Press, 2008).

Campbell, Kurt M. and Michael E. O'Hanlon. *Hard Power: The New Politics of National Security* (New York: Basic Books, 2006).

Darwin, John. *After Tamerlane: The Rise and Fall of Global Empires, 1400–2000* (New York: Penguin, 2008).

Dionne, Jr., E. J. *Why The Right Went Wrong: Conservatism – From Goldwater to the Tea Party and Beyond* (New York: Simon and Schuster, 2016).

Dueck, Colin. *Hard-Line: The Republican Party and US Foreign Policy since WWII* (Princeton, NJ: Princeton University Press, 2010).

The Obama Doctrine: American Grand Strategy Today (New York: Oxford University Press, 2015).

Edelman, Eric S. *Understanding America's Contested Primacy* (Washington, DC: Center for Strategic and Budgetary Assessments, 2010).

Ferguson, Niall. *Colossus: The Rise and Fall of the American Empire* (London: Allen Lane, 2004).

Friedman, George and Meredith LeBard. *The Coming War with Japan* (New York: St. Martin's Press, 1991).

Gelpi, Christopher, Peter D. Feaver and Jason Reifler. *Paying the Human Costs of War: American Public Opinion and Casualties in Military Conflicts* (Princeton, NJ: Princeton University Press, 2009).

Gilpin, Robert. *War and Change in World Politics* (New York: Cambridge University Press,1983).

Gries, Peter Hays. *The Politics of American Foreign Policy: How Ideology Divides Liberals and Conservatives over Foreign Affairs* (Stanford, CA: Stanford University Press, 2014).

Jones, Bruce. *Still Ours to Lead: America, Rising Powers, and the Tension between Rivalry and Restraint* (Washington, DC: Brookings Institution Press, 2014).

Kabaservice, Geoffrey. *Rule and Ruin: The Downfall of Moderation and the Destruction of the Republican Party, from Eisenhower to the Tea Party* (New York: Oxford University Press, 2012).

Kagan, Robert. *Paradise and Power: America and Europe in the New World Order* (London: Atlantic Books, 2003).

The World America Made (New York: Alfred Knopf, 2012).

Kennedy, Paul. *The Rise and Fall of the Great Powers: Economic Change and Military Conflict 1500–2000* (London: Fontana, 1989).

Kissinger, Henry. *World Order: Reflections on the Character of Nations and the Course of History* (London: Allen Lane, 2014).

Mann, Thomas E. and Norman J. Ornstein. *It's Even Worse Than It Looks: How the American Constitutional System Collided with the New Politics of Extremism* (New York: Basic Books, 2012).

Nasr, Vali. *The Dispensable Nation: American Foreign Policy in Retreat* (New York: Doubleday, 2013).

Nye, Joseph. *Is the American Century Over?* (Cambridge, UK: Polity Press, 2015).

Obama, Barack. *The Audacity of Hope: Thoughts on Reclaiming the American Dream* (New York: Crown Publishers, 2006).

Page, Benjamin I. and Marshall M. Bouton. *The Foreign Policy Disconnect: What Americans Want from Our Leaders But Don't Get* (Chicago, IL: University of Chicago Press, 2006).

Panetta, Leon. *Worthy Fights: A Memoir of Leadership in War and Peace* (New York: Penguin Press, 2014).

Paulson, Henry M. *Dealing with China: An Insider Unmasks the New Economic Superpower* (London: Headline, 2015).

Piereson, James. *Shattered Consensus: The Rise and Decline of America's Postwar Political Order* (New York: Encounter Books, 2015).

Posen, Barry. *Restraint: A New Foundation for US Grand Strategy* (Ithaca, NY: Cornell University Press, 2015).

Rynhold, Jonathan. *The Arab-Israeli Conflict in American Political Culture* (New York: Cambridge University Press, 2015).

Singer, P. W. and August Cole. *Ghost Fleet: A Novel of the Next World War* (New York: Houghton Mifflin Harcourt, 2015).

Singh, Robert S. *Barack Obama's Post-American Foreign Policy: The Limits of Engagement* (London: Bloomsbury, 2012).

Sky, Emma. *The Unravelling: High Hopes and Missed Opportunities in Iraq* (London: Atlantic Books, 2015).

Smeltz, Dina, Ivo Daalder, Karl Friedhoff and Craig Kafura. *America Divided: Political Partisanship and US Foreign Policy* (Chicago: The Chicago Council on Global Affairs, 2015).

Tierney, Dominic. *The Right Way to Lose a War: America in an Age of Unwinnable Conflicts* (New York: Little, Brown and Company, 2015).

Updike, John. *Toward the End of Time* (New York: Random House, 1997).

Urban, Mark. *The Edge: Is the Military Dominance of the West Coming to an End?* (New York, London: Little, Brown, 2015).

Yeats, William Butler. *Collected Poems* (London: Picador, 1990).

Zakaria, Fareed. *The Post-American World* (New York: Allen Lane, 2008).

Articles and reports

Allison, Graham. "The Thucydides Trap: Are the US and China Headed for War?" *The Atlantic* September 24, 2015, at: www.theatlantic.com/international/archive/2015/09/united-states-china-war-thucydides-trap/406756/

Brands, Hal. "Fools Rush Out? The Flawed Logic of Offshore Balancing," *The Washington Quarterly* 38 (2) 2015, pp. 7–28.

Brzezinski, Zbigniew. "From Hope to Audacity: Appraising Obama's Foreign Policy," *Foreign Affairs* 89 (1) 2010, pp. 16–30.

Cutler, Lloyd N. "To Form a Government," *Foreign Affairs* 59 (1) 1980, pp. 126–43.

DeYoung, Karen. "Dozens of Retired Generals, Admirals Back Iran Deal," *Washington Post* August 11, 2015, at: www.washingtonpost.com/world/national-security/retired-generals-and-admirals-back-iran-nuclear-deal/2015/08/11/bd26f6ae-4045-11e5-bfe3-ff1d8549bfd2_story.html

Edelman, Eric and Ray Takeyh. "On Iran, Congress Should Just Say No," *Washington Post* July 17, 2015, at: www.washingtonpost.com/opinions/on-iran-congress-should-just-say-no/2015/07/17/56e366ae-2b30-11e5-bd33-395c05608059_story.html

Foster, Peter. "It's Farewell to a Nation of Two Tribes that Scarcely Meet," *Sunday Telegraph* August 9, 2015, p. 16.

Fukuyama, Francis. "America in Decay: The Sources of Political Dysfunction," *Foreign Affairs* 93 (5) 2014, pp. 5–26.

Goldberg, Jeffrey. "Hillary Clinton: 'Failure' to Help Syrian Rebels Led to the Rise of ISIS," *The Atlantic* August 10, 2014, at: www.theatlantic.com/international/archive/2014/08/hillary-clinton-failure-to-help-syrian-rebels-led-to-the-rise-of-isis/375832/

Hammond, David. "Mapped: How the World Became More Violent," *The Daily Telegraph* at: www.telegraph.co.uk/news/worldnews/big-question-kcl/11711266/Mapped-How-the-world-became-more-violent.html

Hof, Frederic C. "America's Self-Inflicted Wound in Syria," *Foreign Policy* August 21, 2015, at: http://foreignpolicy.com/2015/08/21/americas-self-inflicted-wound-in-syria/

Kissinger, Henry A. "A Path Out of the Middle East Collapse," *The Wall Street Journal* October 16, 2015, at: www.wsj.com/articles/a-path-out-of-the-middle-east-collapse-1445037513

Kristof, Nicholas. "U.S.A., Land of Limitations?" *The New York Times* Sunday Review August 8, 2015.

Kroenig, Matthew. "Facing Reality: Getting NATO Ready for a New Cold War," *Survival* 57 (1) 2015, pp. 49–70.

Kupchan, Charles A. and Peter L. Trubowitz. "The Illusion of Liberal Internationalism's Revival," *International Security* 35 (1) 2010, pp. 95–109.

Lettow, Paul. "Have We Hit Peak America? The Sources of US Power and the Path to National Renaissance," *Foreign Policy* July/August 2014, pp. 54–63, at: http://foreignpolicy.com/2014/07/03/have-we-hit-peak-america/

Mandelbaum, Michael. "How to Prevent an Iranian Bomb: The Case for Deterrence," *Foreign Affairs* 94 (6) 2015, pp. 19–24.

  "Nuclear Arms Control, Then and Now," *The American Interest* April 22, 2015, at: www.the-american-interest.com/2015/04/22/nuclear-arms-control-then-and-now/

Manning, Jennifer E. *The 114th Congress: A Profile* (Washington, DC: CRS Report 7-5700, June 11, 2015).

Nincic, Miroslav and Monti Narayan Datta. "Of Paradise, Power, and Pachyderms," *Political Science Quarterly* 122 (2) 2007, pp. 239–56.

O'Hanlon, Michael. "Obama's Military Policy: Down-Size While Threats Rise," *The Wall Street Journal* October 28, 2015, at www.wsj.com/article_email/obamas-military-policy-down-size-while-threats-rise-1446073142-lMyQjAx MTE1MzIxOTIyOTk4Wj

O'Keefe, Ed. "Jeb Bush: Obama and Clinton's Iraq Withdrawal 'Premature' and a 'Fatal Error'," *Washington Post* August 11, 2015, at: www.washingtonpost.com/news/post-politics/wp/2015/08/11/jeb-bush-obama-and-clintons-iraq-withdrawal-premature-and-a-fatal-error/?wpisrc=nl_daily202&wpmm=1

Pollack, Kenneth M. and Ray Takeyh. "Near Eastern Promises: Why Washington Should Focus on the Middle East," *Foreign Affairs* 93 (3) 2014, pp. 92–105.

Rothkopf, David. "The Curse of the Obama Doctrine," *Foreign Policy* September 3, 2015, at: http://foreignpolicy.com/2015/09/03/the-curse-of-the-obama-doctrine-middle-east- arab-world/

Rubio, Marco. "Restoring America's Strength: My Vision for America," *Foreign Affairs* 94 (5) 2015, pp. 108–15.

Takeyh, Ray. "The Payoff for Iran," *Washington Post* June 28, 2015, at: www.washingtonpost.com/opinions/the-payoff-for-iran/2015/06/28/6c8d58ac-1c26-11e5-bd7f-4611a60dd8e5_story.html?hpid=z7

Webb, Justin. "Americans Warn Europe: You're on Your Own," *The Times* June 12, 2015, p. 24.

Index